MW00912443

LOOSE SCREWS

by Gerry Tortorelli

Certified
Author's First Print Run
October 26, 2009

106/191

Signed   Numbered

Loose Screws

*Anecdotes from a Bronx boy who
has lived around the world*

GERRY TORTORELLI

iUniverse, Inc.
New York   Bloomington

Loose Screws
Anecdotes from a Bronx boy who has lived around the world

Copyright © 2009 Gerard Tortorelli

All rights reserved. No part of this book may be used or reproduced by any means, graphic, electronic, or mechanical, including photocopying, recording, taping or by any information storage retrieval system without the written permission of the publisher except in the case of brief quotations embodied in critical articles and reviews.

The views expressed in this work are solely those of the author and do not necessarily reflect the views of the publisher, and the publisher hereby disclaims any responsibility for them.

iUniverse books may be ordered through booksellers or by contacting:

iUniverse
1663 Liberty Drive
Bloomington, IN 47403
www.iuniverse.com
1-800-Authors (1-800-288-4677)

Because of the dynamic nature of the Internet, any Web addresses or links contained in this book may have changed since publication and may no longer be valid. The views expressed in this work are solely those of the author and do not necessarily reflect the views of the publisher, and the publisher hereby disclaims any responsibility for them.

ISBN: 978-1-4401-7069-0 (pbk)
ISBN: 978-1-4401-7067-6 (cloth)
ISBN: 978-1-4401-7068-3 (ebk)

Printed in the United States of America

iUniverse rev. date: 9/30/2009

Dedication

For Susan, my best friend

Acknowledgments

Hugs and kisses to the Queen, who puts up with me
while I write things in my head, way before they go on paper.

Thank you to Gary Larson, who helped me through this book-writing odyssey.

A big thank you to Sue Ducharme who edited my manuscript with style
and a human touch while keeping it true to my voice.

Thank you to the already published Ginny McMorrow and Victoria
Morey, who encouraged me to join their ranks.

Thank you to the princesses, serfs, siblings, parents, in-laws, cousins,
friends, and colleagues who have made the journey worthwhile.

And to Mr. Dooney, that mythical character, wherever you may be.

Table of Contents

The Premise

Some funny things happened between the Bronx and now

I believe life is what one perceives it to be, and I try to perceive humor in life at all times. I laugh therefore I am. (Apologies to Mr. Descartes.)

This book presents a collection of the episodes and people that have made my journey so much fun. Some are in far-off lands, some around the corner. You will experience them through the eyes of a Bronx kid who has lived and worked outside of the United States for twenty-one years.

I spent the 1950s and '60s living on East 222 Street in Our Lady of Grace parish. My schooling from kindergarten through college took place in the Bronx. Okay, the master's degree was obtained in New Haven, but at the time that seemed to be the farthest that I would ever go.

Upon graduation from Manhattan College, which is in the Bronx, not Manhattan, I moved with my new wife to the far reaches of the world—translation: Waterbury, Connecticut. Although a mere seventy-five miles from my home, it might as well have been the end of the world. New Yorkers are funny like that. As cosmopolitan as we would like to consider ourselves, we really only know and care about our immediate neighborhoods. Our East 222 Street crowd would pack a lunch if we had to go past 230 Street. To venture to New Jersey probably meant one needed a passport.

So you can imagine our friends and family's shock when we moved to Switzerland in 1981 with our two young daughters. Our new home, about thirty miles north of Zürich, was a small town in the German-speaking part of the country. Altikon had 472 inhabitants, and we were the only foreigners.

The result of the original two-year assignment was that we finally came back to the States sixteen years later. During that time, we lived in both the German-speaking and French-speaking parts of Switzerland, in Ontario, Canada, and in England. When we finally got back to the United States, we landed in Solon, Ohio, a suburb of Cleveland. Even our last stint here in Ohio had an international twist, since for part it,

I lived in Ohio while my office was back in Switzerland. That was a hell of a commute—great for airline mile points.

All these relocations were predicated by my job. I started out as a chemical engineer for a rubber company, then moved into the food industry, where I held positions in research, technical sales, marketing, and general management. I even ran a joint venture in the healthcare field for a while.

Throughout all of this, our family has seen wondrous things, met great people, picked up another nationality, and simply experienced day-to-day life as it happened.

The reader will share the anecdotes though my eyes. If I believe what some of my friends tell me, I have a weird way of looking at the world. But don't worry; you don't need a loose screw to understand the book, although it might help.

Read, enjoy, and, most of all, laugh.

1. Life before the monarchy

As I said, I spent the 1950s and '60s living on East 222 Street in Our Lady of Grace parish, and from kindergarten through college, my schooling took place in the Bronx. Times were simpler then, and exotic places like Europe existed only in geography class.

The sister who doesn't clean

We took vitamins as kids. I don't remember what brand they were—probably a generic type: round, bright yellow-orange pills. They weren't made to resemble stone-age cartoon characters. They came in a very large amber-colored bottle. This was one of the things that my family bought in bulk. I am not sure how many came in a bottle, but I think the quantity was written on the label in scientific notation. My parents had not studied the amount of B-12 or zinc in them. They were just told to give their kids some vitamins, so they went out and got some. Times were simpler then.

Maybe it was the amber-colored bottle that gave them their mystique; maybe it was because they were supposed to do magic things to our bodies; or maybe it was that our parents bemoaned the fact that these were expensive, but those pills had a very special place in our psyches.

One morning, Laura, the younger of my two sisters, and I were up early and went to take our vitamins. As she was eight and I was six, our hands were not as big as needed to handle this massive bottle. So one of us—I can't remember who—spilled the entire bottle onto the kitchen floor.

Usually if I can't remember who it was and it was something bad, I claim it was the other person. So let's just say my sister spilled all these yellow-orange pills, and I was just an observer. Laura has been a nurse for thirty-five years now. I sometimes wonder if she spills pills at the hospital too. Maybe her nurse nickname is "Dropsy." I'll ask her the next time I see her.

Laura is now a grandmother. That is shocking to me, as she was the renegade of the family. Don't get me wrong—she wasn't a hippie, and she didn't drop acid every ten minutes. Being a renegade in our family was not as renegade-like as in other families. She was the partier, the one that pushed the envelope. She was, in a word, normal.

I once heard one of my mother's friends comment that she thought my sister and her friends kept their bra straps too tight and wore sweaters that were way too small. This was said in a tone that conveyed that this deserved excommunication at the least. I thought it deserved sainthood myself and vowed that if I ever became pope I would make one of the saints the patron of tight sweaters.

Near the end of her life, my mother had an extended convalescence period that kept her out of her own house for almost six months. Both of my sisters kept on eye on my mother's house.

I was in New York the week that Mom came home for the first time. Laura and I were staying with her. The second evening Mom started asking us where a number of her favorite things were and why some of the pictures had been rearranged on her picture table. At first we shrugged this off, answering that as people cleaned the house in her absence they just moved things into different places. After being asked a few more times, Laura said she had not moved anything. Finally after being grilled a few more times, Laura answered, "Look, Ma, I'm not the daughter who cleans, remember. Your other daughter cleans."

She had a point. In my opinion, Laura has a healthy attitude towards cleaning. My sister Margaret, however, is a bit of a fanatic. Margaret had in fact cleaned my mother's empty house, which seemed to me to be a waste of time, but everyone needs a passion in life. Margaret has three: cleaning, teaching, and picking on Joey, my brother-in-law. He is already a saint, the official patron of being married to a cleaner. I'm not sure if the Catholic Church has recognized this yet, but he will get his reward one day.

As it turns out, Margaret may now be the only true cleaner in the family, but in 1956 we were all cleaners. My mother had made us all cleaners. Not that we actually cleaned; that was Mom's domain. We were simply taught that cleaning was a sacred calling. So when something spilled, you cleaned it up—for instance, a bottle of vitamins.

Back in 1956, the loneliest creature in the world would have been a germ on my mother's kitchen floor. So spilling a bottle of vitamins was not a big issue. All you needed to do was pick them up. It's funny how things that seem so simple now just sort of eluded us then.

One of the sacred credos of neatness fanatics is that if it falls on the floor, it can never be eaten—no five-second rule at all. This is counter-intuitive; since neatniks have clean floors, if something falls you most likely could eat it. Slobs have dirty floors, so if something touches the floor you shouldn't eat it, though slobs probably do. My mother's floor was so clean that you could time the five-second rule with a calendar and not a stopwatch. Still, if something fell, the rule was it was to be discarded.

Laura and I were mortified when we spilled the vitamins on the kitchen floor. First of all, they were quite expensive, and secondly, what would happen to us if we couldn't take our vitamins? We might not live until evening. There was no way we could eat them, however, after they hit the floor. Mom had trained us well.

So what would an eight- and six-year-old do? How about wash them? Sounds good, but how? I will claim that using the colander was my idea, but it could have been Laura's. A colander is a great multi-use tool. Strain spaghetti by night, wash pills by day. Throw them in, run some tap water over them, and, presto, you have clean vitamin pills.

You might envision us putting the colander in the sink and using the spray nozzle on one of those retractable rubber hoses to wash them. You would be wrong. This was 1956, and we didn't have a spray nozzle on a retractable rubber hose. Pure and simple, we had the faucet. Like the channel 2 through 13 twist dial on our old TV, a faucet was all we had. So we had to run the water and shake the colander to achieve distribution.

You know that bright yellow-orange color I mentioned in the first paragraph? Well, it fast changed to a dull yellow color under water. The water that left the colander was quite pretty, however, a sort of vitamin-coating soup. Here's the important moral so far: Vitamins don't like being washed. They get really sticky. So we had a one-pound, semi-yellow snowball of sticky pills. This was not working out as we had planned.

Our deduction: If only they weren't wet, we might be able to salvage most of them. Let's see, how does one dry wet, sticky pills? You are probably thinking hand-held hair dryer. I would too, except this was 1956, and if they had been invented, we didn't have one—sort of like the retractable rubber nozzle.

The next best thing was the oven. So we spread the very sticky, light yellow pills onto a cookie sheet and put them into the oven for fifteen minutes. Trust me, no cookbooks give the time and temperature for drying wet vitamins, so like most everything else in this saga, we improvised. Funny how these things can get out of hand very quickly.

Suffice it to say, none of those pills were salvaged. Well, that may be an overstatement. The two pills we were supposed to take that morning, we took. At least we didn't waste the current day's allotment of vitamins.

That in itself wasn't such a good idea, since by the time we ate them, the yellow-orange covering was completely gone. Besides making the pills look nice, the yellow-orange covering was there to protect the vitamins from the ravages of air and moisture. It was also there to protect your tongue from the ravages of the taste of the vitamins. These were indeed bitter pills to swallow.

This was a great learning experience. I got to see that a vitamin pill is not yellow-orange throughout. I learned that once you dissolve a pill's coating, it's hard to put it back. And I think this was when my sister Laura became the sister who doesn't clean. We are all products of our experiences.

Chiffon pie

I have a friend whom I have known for over fifty years. She was a classmate in grammar school. I know her as Marie, while my sisters know her as Chrissy. I know her middle name is Christine, but why my family knows her by a different name than I do is a mystery. I have to ask her next time we talk.

For some reason, in fifth grade we found ourselves with adjacent desks. Most likely, the nuns put us together because we were both good students, or maybe it was that both our mothers were active in the school. I have no idea. I only know that we sat next to each other.

With our adjacent desks, we had a lot of time to chat and share ideas. Marie was always more intelligent than I, but if she is reading this, I deny ever saying that—the female editors put it in.

Being in the upper quartile of smartness in the class, both of us became quickly bored with what was going on. I figure we must have been geniuses, since at that time the nuns taught only to the smart kids. If you were dumb, you were left out. So if we were bored and the nuns were exclusively teaching to the smart kids, we certainly were geniuses.

It became clear that we needed to occupy our time with other pursuits. We decided to re-write the history of World War II, with both of us playing major roles. In fact, I can hear good old Winston now: "Never before have so many owed so much to Marie and Gerard." Or maybe he said "Chrissy and Gerard." I'll have to check my history books.

I am guessing that this type of endeavor was more my doing than hers, because it is the young boy who falls in love with war and not normally the young girl. In a few short years a land we never knew existed called Vietnam would change our imaginary view of war and with it end the innocence we shared in the fifth grade.

In addition to saving the world, Marie and I had other things in common. We both have at least one older sister. I have two; she has one. In our earliest years, we were both Girl Scouts.

In the '50s it was not common to get a babysitter for your kids, at least not in our family. My mother took the kids along wherever she went or she didn't go. Remember, I had two older sisters. They were both Girl Scouts, as was Marie's older sister. I also recall both our mothers being Girl Scout leaders or at least assisting the leaders. What could my mother do with me, the lone son, while they were off at their meetings? Well, take him along. I was sort of the tagalong younger brother. When I was old enough, I joined the boy's version of the Scouts, but this only lasted a short while, as none of my friends were that into it. Besides, they didn't have the cookies.

Marie and I stayed friends. She introduced me to comic genius of Tom Lehrer. She also introduced me to my first girlfriend.

In high school, Marie decided to have a costume party one Halloween for a small group: the six kids we hung around with and a few others. At age fifteen, boys aren't very comfortable dressing up when girls are present, so a lot of thought went into my costume. To this day, I don't remember what I wore. What I do remember is that the hostess apparently did not come in costume.

I was mad. Marie invited us to this party, we dressed up in costumes with girls present, and she didn't even wear one. I felt betrayed. Okay, this sounds a little melodramatic, but it helps make my point. In hindsight, I guess I could have considered that maybe she was dressed as her alter ego, Chrissy.

Partway into the party, someone asked Marie why she hadn't worn a costume to her own party. I thought that a bold question, but you have to know the guy who asked it. Marie said, without batting an eye,

"Oh, but I am in costume." As we all stared in amazement and tried to figure out what her costume was, she pointed to a pi symbol (π) she had pinned to her chiffon dress. She had come as a chiffon pie. I told you she was smarter than me. Sorry, smarter than I.

In later years when I was running a company and gave management talks, I once mentioned the chiffon pie dress story to my audience. In business today, it is all too common for people to try to wow you with some idea or product. They stick it right in your face, give you all the info, whether you want it or not: the hard sell. Marie had the confidence and discipline to let her costume be revealed at the right moment. I can't tell you what I wore, what Stevie or John wore, or even what the other girls wore, but I will never forget Marie's chiffon pie.

I laughed recently when I found my old management speech notes. The title of this particular section was, "Speak softly but wear a chiffon dress." Words to live by.

"It is balloon!" [1]

Claire is the oldest within our high school group of friends. She was born in February, 1950. All the other friends in our immediate group were born later that year. She is the oldest. This is something she does not necessarily bring up in conversation now, but back in 1968, she was the first one to hit the magic eighteen. In New York State in 1968, eighteen-year-olds could legally drink.

There was no option but to have a party, a surprise party. It was to be at my house. I remember that about fifteen kids were invited. Someone got the idea to suspend a large number of balloons from the very high ceiling in our living room and we would let them all fall at a certain time.

We found various sources for balloons. We really didn't care what they looked like. There were the long thin ones, round ones, even a few heart-shaped ones, and of course the "Mickey Mouse" type, consisting

---

1   Title taken from a line in an episode of the TV show, *F Troop* (Season 2, Episode 3: *Bye, Bye Balloon*). Chief Wild Eagle, played by Frank DeKova, sees a hot air balloon in the sky and yells, "It is balloon!" What would he have yelled in my living room?

of a head with two ears. They came in blue, white, yellow, green, and the all-important, as we found out later, pink.

Now it took a while to blow up all these balloons. The five of us planning the party—Marie, Joanne, John, Stevie and myself—did the work. Okay, I will admit that my dad actually did much of the balloon inflation. He seemed to enjoy it. If I recall correctly, we had around 170 balloons.

Once inflated, we threw them into the string net that we had constructed to hold them below the ceiling, just above our heads. This wasn't a real net, just strings we had tied together and attached to the "master string" that ran along one wall. At the right moment, we would pull the "master string" and all the balloons would fall onto the unsuspecting dancers. We had decided the best option was during a slow dance. With an eleven-foot ceiling, we had a few spare feet to use for balloons. Did I mention we had a lot of balloons?

The space between adjacent strings was about eight inches, so some balloons actually fell through and others were partially suspended through the spaces, hanging there above our heads. We had to place them carefully.

Marie reminded me recently that John and she did the actual design and construction of this string system. She remembered that at one point Joanne was in charge of escorting Stevie and I to the store to buy the soda. It seems we had to get out of the house in order to allow the master design team to complete their job. Evidently, Stevie and I were not being helpful; we were "having too much fun." Joanne must have done her job well, since Marie and John got their job done, and we had a homemade string-balloon-retention system in my living room.

We figured only a hand full of the balloons would deflate by the Saturday night party. Some actually deflated rather quickly. That is when we noticed an odd thing about balloons. As they deflate, the ends contract and get darker, while the very tip goes back to the original shape. If you can imagine, let's say ... a nipple and the surrounding areola?

This was especially noticeable with the mouse-eared balloons. As they deflated, the ears became small enough to fall through alternate spaces in our homemade net, though the head kept them from falling all the way through. It was starting to look like we had a whole lot of multi-colored breasts hanging down from the ceiling. The pink ones were especially realistic.

Once we noticed this, it seemed we got tired of the inflation job. We never seemed to be able to completely inflate the mouse-eared balloons. They started out with nipples. Remember this was 1968, and we were a lot more innocent then. Did I mention the pink ones were especially realistic?

Thirty-eight years later, you would not think that the group would remember much of that evening. The truth of the matter is that we indeed remember a lot about that evening, but we all remember a different facet of it. In fact, there seems to be great correlation among the girls and great correlation among the guys, but no correlation between the two groups.

Claire's, Marie's and Joanne's recollections (a summary of a conversation in 2006): singing "George of the Jungle" that morning while setting up the balloons; my dad blowing up the balloons and happy to be part of our process; Claire being very surprised and overwhelmed; Joanne leading Stevie and Gerry on a soda shopping trip to get us "out of the way;" the balloons not falling all at once—it took a while for some of them to come down; the popping of the balloons when they finally did come down.

John, Stevie, and Gerry's sole recollection: Tons and tons of tits hanging from the ceiling.

The Ripple effect

Volumes have been written about the effect of birth order within a family. I have never read any of these, but I am sure that the third and last-born is deemed to be the most intelligent, sexiest, and most charming of all. Did I mention that I am the youngest of three?

Whether family birth order has as big an impact as some say, I have no idea. I do know, however, that it is always good to have an older friend. Especially when you are seventeen and the drinking age is eighteen.

Of our group of three guys in high school, Stevie was born in May. I am a July baby, and John was useless with an October birthday.

Remember this was 1968, when the drinking age in New York State was eighteen.

This meant that after May 26, 1968, Stevie could legally buy the alcohol for our outings. He may have had the right to purchase liquor, but none of us really understood what we were buying. Case in point: We decided to spike a watermelon during prom week. Having no idea what to do, we bought a bottle of gin. I think we most likely did this because it was a clear liquid. We figured it was alcohol, plain and simple. Imagine the combination of tastes: watermelon with the gin flavor—not very appealing.

Even applying the gin to the fruit was a bit of a disaster. My sister, who loved to lead me down the path to ruin, was a nursing student, so she supplied us with hypodermic needles, with which we intended to inject the gin into the melon. Of course, the needle holes in the hard-skinned melon did not heal very well, so the gin leaked out all over my mother's kitchen table. We finally ended up taking one end off the melon, turning it on its other end, and sticking the bottle in it upside down—a sort of perverted hourglass effect. We did have some success with the needles on oranges, since citrus does seem to heal up pretty well.

We had other interesting teenage alcohol experiences as well. At that time, I lived on East 222nd Street while John lived on East 228th Street. The liquor store was between 224th and 225th. John had invited us over to watch *A Man for All Seasons* one evening. Stevie met me at the liquor store, and we bought a pint of the old standard, Seagram 7. We had to kill some time until John's parents were out of the house, so we started drinking it on the way. I guess we were very thirsty, because all the liquor was gone by the time we made the three-block walk.

As a result, we arrived at John's house feeling no pain. This was not exactly what John wanted, since he was very intent on watching the movie. It was clear by the first commercial that Stevie and I were not going to be quiet enough for John to enjoy this classic. John, being the gracious host, offered to make us a drink. We readily accepted. On the second commercial, John put a shot of every liquor he could find in his father's liquor cabinet in two glasses and served them to us. Stevie and I downed these quite quickly, never noticing that John was not drinking at all. By the time that the fourth commercial was being aired, we decided we should leave. We didn't want to redecorate John's mother's carpets.

I don't really remember how Stevie made out that night, but I lost my lunch on the steps of our grammar school, Our Lady of Grace. When I say I don't remember how Stevie did, it isn't the years that have passed that have dimmed my memory; I had no recollection of what happened the next day either.

It was later in that summer, when we were together in my backyard, that John's day came. We were poor, bound-for-college kids, and all we could afford was six bottles of Ripple. For those of you under fifty, I must explain that Ripple was a wine that cost about 59 cents per bottle at the time. For some reason, John happened to be very thirsty that night and downed the wine rather quickly. We were making toasts to various things: parts of women's bodies, etc. Just good ole, wholesome teenage stuff. Although Stevie and I were tipsy, John was totally gone.

Even in his state, John was already devoted to his future career as an environmental engineer in the wastewater treatment field. Stevie and I could tell this by the intensity with which he was studying the water in our toilet bowl. To make sure we all realized he was doing some type of fieldwork, he would, from time to time, make what I can only describe as very loud, gut-wrenching sounds.

I am not sure why we did what we did next, but we decided that John could not go home the way he was. His parents would not appreciate his condition. Stevie and I came to the conclusion that we should give him a shower before he went home: the water kind, not the party kind. My old home on East 222nd Street had a shower stall, which was novel for a house built in 1933.

So there we were in a rather small bathroom, with John au naturelle, guiding him into the shower. I don't remember much about getting him undressed, and even if I did, I wouldn't admit it. He did have a Ripple label pasted on his chest. That man had brand loyalty. By the way, at that time John was a "brief" guy, not a "boxer" guy. The next time we talk, I'll have to ask him what he wears now.

We learned a lot that evening. Some things were very useful. For instance, if you have a drunk friend sitting on the floor of a shower stall with water cascading over his body, making everything wet and slippery, and he asks for a drink of water, do not give him a glass. The odds of him dropping it on the ceramic tile are quite high, resulting in a sickening sound of glass shattering, followed by one of his friends yelling, "Don't move or you will cut your balls off!"

We finished the shower without any damage to our friend or his privates. Once he was out of the shower, it was necessary for someone to dry him. I really have no recollection of who did what, but since I am writing the story, I will claim categorically that Stevie dried John all over with a very nice green towel that my mother had on the rack. Hey, when Stevie writes his version, he can have me drying John. It's called poetic license.

There John was, all clean and dry and ready to go home. Stevie and I had now stopped most of our laughing and were almost coherent, when my mother arrived home with my two cousins, identical twins. John took one look and thought he was seeing double. Stevie and I went nuts again and couldn't stop laughing for what seemed to be hours.

I am still not sure why this cheap wine went to John's head so quickly when it didn't affect Stevie and me in the same way. He claims it had to do with the fact that he had worked all day with nothing to eat. Maybe that's true, but John is the oldest in his family, while Stevie and I are both the youngest of three. Maybe birth order does matter after all.

Simon Peter, the fisherman

I hope you are not expecting this piece to have a biblical theme. I just chose the name because I thought it sounded good. Well, that and it *is* about a guy named Peter and his fishing exploits. The Simon part is pure embellishment.

I have a first cousin who is one year younger than I. His name is Peter. Since he was born on the 16th of July and I on the 18th the previous year, we are the same age for two full days. We grew up not too far from each other in the Bronx. He was best man at my wedding. He and his younger brother, Victor, went to the same college as I did. We saw a lot of each other.

When Peter and I were in college, my brother-in-law, Joe, introduced both of us to fishing. Of course, after we went once we figured that we could do this all on our own. We would either hire a small rowboat, sometimes with a motor, or fish from the shore. In the fish-catching category, we had some good days and some bad days, but we always had lots of fun. There was the day we caught fourteen blue fish while trolling in Long Island Sound. This bounty prompted Victor to exclaim, "You must have hit a herd!" The guy may be a chemistry genius, but he knows little, it seems, about *schools* of fish.

Fresh water anglers have it easy. I know they complain about us salt-water guys having less finesse than they do, but we have to deal with something that they never even consider: the tides. In particular, I remember one day when Peter and I decided we would rent a rowboat and go out on the bay that lies between Jones Beach and the main part of Long Island.

The man at the rental shack was adamant that by no means were we to take the boat under the causeway bridge. He mentioned this two or three times while we were getting our gear together. Both Peter and I, having attended Catholic high school, knew how to take an order, so we had no intention of going anywhere near the causeway bridge.

Our intent was simply to row out a few hundred yards and bottom-fish. I think we were after flounder on that afternoon. I guess a number of people had the same idea, because soon six or seven boats were in this small inlet. We certainly had plenty of room but, you know, a fisherman always likes to be alone with nature. We therefore decided to row farther out and get into the main section of the larger bay. Then we decided to move toward the east end of the bay to find a special spot all our own. The rowing was actually quite easy. There seemed to be a small current helping us along. Imagine that, a current out there? We decided to let the boat just drift.

Soon we were having a great time. Not too many nibbles, but we had our sand worms and our sodas, and we were enjoying the sun. A boat a hundred yards from us caught an eel. We both decided we would not be happy catching an eel. We told each other that was because neither one of our mothers knew how to cook eel. In actuality it was because neither one of us wanted to take it off the hook.

After some small talk and re-baiting our hooks a few times, we noticed that we were now all by ourselves in the eastern side of the bay. In fact, we were getting more and more eastern every moment. It was then we realized that the tide had been going out all the while.

If you are so inclined, you can calculate how fast the water was moving. All you need to know is the surface area of the bay, the water height at high tide, the height at low tide, the approximate time the tide takes to go out, and, of course, the area that the water was flowing through. These are the type of things Peter and I would discuss, he being a physics major and me being an engineering student. I think we probably decided that the solution required a differential equation, as the rate of flow was non-constant. I challenge any of my fresh water friends to have this type of discussion while wading around in some stagnant lake.

Regardless of what type of equation we needed, we soon came to the realization that all this water, and there was a lot, was emptying from the bay through one small channel. In layman's terms, the physics goes like this: When a lot of water goes throw a small opening, it goes pretty fast. To make matters worse, the small channel that all this water was going through led right under the causeway bridge. You know, the one that we were warned about: "Do not go under the causeway bridge."

It became clear as well that our little puny anchor was not really holding us at all. I guess it might have if we used it before we started moving as fast as we were. So there we were, heading for the causeway bridge. The good news was that we had enough height to get under it without being decapitated. The bad news was we were definitely going under the bridge.

Usually when unavoidable things like this happen, your intuition is to sit back and let them happen. This was not one of those times for Peter. As we were passing under the bridge, he had the idea that if he grabbed onto the piling he could hold the boat from going under the bridge. I can still see this as if it were yesterday. The bridge stayed where it was, the boat kept on moving, and Peter started to look like a rubberband man in a cartoon. He let go just as he was about to hit the water. The boat, rocking back and forth, shot under the dreaded causeway bridge into the calm water of the bay on the other side.

We were still alive and decided we should beach the boat and regroup. The rest of the day was spent fishing from the shore on the wrong side of the causeway bridge while we waited for the tide to turn so we could row back under the bridge. Even though we didn't catch anything, we did see the largest horseshoe crab I have ever seen, so the day was not a complete waste.

We ended up with nothing to take home but a story of courage and daring, differential equations, and sea monsters posing as eels. It became the "Saga of the Causeway Bridge." We also came away with the strong conviction that the next time we would pay extra for a boat with a motor.

We did, in fact, do that the following trip, which was for black fish in Long Island Sound. But that is not without problems either, especially if you try to start the motor in very shallow water. We learned all about shear pins and broken propellers that day.

2. Enter the Queen

My wife is the Queen,
it is she I must obey.
My daughters are the princesses,
they too have their say.
And I, I am a serf
and would have it no other way
(or at least I tell myself that).

Piña coladas and the rest of my life

One of the great things about marrying your high school sweetheart is that you get to discover so much together. I used to say "one of my high school sweethearts" because I did date other girls in high school, but my Queen suggested that I alter that statement, pointing out that she was the only real *sweetheart*. I don't argue with the Queen about this type of thing.

We discovered something delightful on our honeymoon: piña coladas. We honeymooned in Saint Thomas in 1972. At that time, piña coladas were not that well known in our section of the Bronx. Come to think of it, we didn't have many palm trees either.

On the first night in Saint Thomas, we both choose piña coladas as a cocktail. They were great. The next night at dinner, I decided immediately on another piña colada. Why mess with success? The queen decided on a zombie. (Notice the use of the lowercase *q*; this was the honeymoon, and I did not fully understand what *Queen* meant yet.) After one sip, I realized I had made the right drink choice. What could be better: a new bride, a tropical island, a great dinner, and an exotic cocktail.

After the queen's first taste, she decided that the zombie was not to her liking. She would drink it, but she wasn't that enthusiastic about it. I ask you, men, what would you do on your honeymoon? I offered to switch drinks. This made her very happy and gained me some points. Not that I needed points at that stage, but they were points in any case.

The next evening, I ordered … a piña colada, and the small *q* queen ordered a rum punch. Although she did not say anything, I could tell that I was supposed to ask her if she wanted to switch again. I did ask. We did switch. I consoled myself with the fact that it is a good thing for your bride to be adventurous on her honeymoon.

I will not make the reader go through the litany of alcoholic concoctions that I drank during the rest of the stay, none of which I ordered, by the way. I did get one reprieve when we went to place where the banana daiquiri was invented. We both ordered them. She didn't like it, but I had the same drink so switching would not work.

I used to think that it was just by chance that the queen did not like any of the things she ordered, but I am not that sure now. I think it was a plot. Maybe all along she loved rum punch and zombies. Maybe this was all a conspiracy to teach the new hubby who the Queen really was. (Notice the capital *Q*.) It is probably written up in those women's magazines, like *Cosmo*. Hey, come to think of it, a Cosmo is a very popular drink these days with the Queen and her curling friends. This is further proof of the conspiracy. Even the Warren Commission would have found this one.

Whether it was planned or not, a trend was started that week in July 1972. The Queen has no qualms about experimenting with any menu item as long as I order something she likes. She is not that adventurous, just armed with the certainty that I will switch with her. I have even seen her reconsider her choice once she finds out I am ordering something she doesn't like. It goes something like this:

Queen to waiter: "I'll have the monkey brains stewed in kidney broth."

Me to waiter: "I'll have the tripe." (The Queen hates tripe.)

Queen back to waiter: "Oh, on second thought, I'll have the pot roast."

Happens every time! I can't tell you how many times I have ordered tripe after having heard her order something I won't like. I have actually gotten to like tripe—or at least I tell myself so.

Italians, Germans, and Irish

As I saw it in 1975, I would never be the best man at a wedding. I had no brothers, and my close male friends either had brothers or friends who were closer to them than I was. I was destined never to be the best man at a wedding and therefore never to give a wedding toast.

That's what I thought. Then along came my brother-in-law, the Queen's lone sibling. He asked me to be his best man. I was going to make a wedding toast after all.

The responsibility weighed heavily on me, partly because I wanted to do well by the married couple but also because I knew this was going to be my only chance. I went through speech books, asked friends, and seemed to use reams of paper developing my thoughts.

I remember that I wanted my toast to have three characteristics. It must be relevant to this couple, not some off-the-shelf canned saying.

It must be either deep or funny. And, lastly, it must, and I mean *must*, be memorable.

I have to admit that if you wanted to have a better couple to toast, I don't know who it would be. Both my brother-in-law, Jim, and his wife, Carol, are fun people. They were out to have a good time at their wedding.

By the wedding weekend, I had two toasts in mind. One was very deep and meaningful and might even bring tears to a few people's eyes. The other was a bit more risqué and, if I do say so myself, quite funny. I hemmed and hawed on which one to use. I tested both toasts out on a good friend. He was shocked that I would even consider the funny one. "A wedding is no place for a toast like that!" were his exact words.

So there I was, with two toasts. Somewhere between the church and the reception, I asked the just-married couple if I should use a funny toast or a serious toast. They both said the fun one. To my shame, I had decided on the serious one. I say *shame*, since I really wanted to do the fun one, but I was a bit worried that it would be too rude. I didn't have the guts to do what I wanted. That's the shame, not living up to your vision.

The fun one, the one I didn't choose, started out with the words: "There are a lot of Italians here tonight ..." My brother-in-law's wife is 100 percent Italian heritage, while the Queen and her brother are of Irish-German descent.

There was some drinking by the bridal party before we got to the toast. This may have been enough to loosen me up. I'm not sure, but I'll blame it on the drink. There I was, at the podium ready to make my serious toast, when I heard the words come out of my mouth: "There are a lot of Italians here tonight ..." I started the wrong toast. To this day I have no idea what the other toast was, but I do remember that once I said those words there was no going back. It would have made no sense.

I toasted my Irish-German brother-in-law and his Italian wife with these words.

"There are a lot of Italians here tonight, and a lot of Germans and Irish. Since Jim and Carol represent these nationalities. I therefore toast them as follows: May your spaghetti be al dente, may your corn beef be lean, and may your knockwurst be long and hard."

Memorable... don't you think?

Peppered meat balls

Cooking healthy is not something new in our family. From the very beginning of our marriage, the Queen and I have tried to make foods that are healthful and tasty. I would agree that today we are more sensitive to healthful cooking than thirty-seven years ago. Age will do that to you. In some way or other, however, we have always been health-conscious.

Take a traditional favorite, meatballs. From the onset of our marriage, we inserted a broiling step in their preparation. This allows some of the fat to drip off into the broiling pan, leaving less to find its way into the sauce and, ultimately, our veins. Today it is easier to find lean chop meat, so this may not be as critical as it was when all we could find and afford were the high-fat products. Broiling also gives a roasted flavor to the sauce that we particularly like.

The process is simple and adds little effort, save for cleaning the broiling pan. It does add some time to the preparation, of which you must be aware. Normally we would have the sauce at a low simmer while the broiling is going on. Right after the meatballs are removed from the broiler, they go into the sauce.

I say "we," but in truth at that time in our marriage, I was not the chef in our house. I did cook some but not to the extent that I do now. In fact, the making of meatballs was the Queen's domain. Today the Queen is still the meatball tsar, since I prefer Bolognese sauce. It sticks to the pasta better. These days, whoever gets to the chop meat first gets to make what she (or he) wants.

In any event, the Queen has always been quite proud of the results of her meatball efforts. They always turn out great. The seasoning has to be just right, their size just so, and the simmering done the proper amount of time for flavor development.

As we were both working during the early years, the weekends found us doing many chores, and multi-tasking was the unused name of the game. On one such occasion in 1973, the meatball preparation was taking on added intensity because we were preparing them for guests who were to arrive that evening. While we cleaned the house, the meatballs were put into the oven to broil and so were finished broiling prior to the sauce even being started. The meatballs were put on the stovetop, still in the broiler pan, to await the preparation of the sauce. The Queen was attending to the laundry while I was vacuuming.

I have to admit that those fully cooked meatballs were very tempting. Maybe she wouldn't miss just one. I had eaten a good breakfast, but the mid-morning hunger pangs were just setting in. The smell of the broiling meat also heightened my appetite. I decided to let sleeping meatballs lie and go about my chores and forget about the tasty morsels on top of the stove. That's why I thought the Queen was clairvoyant when a few minutes later she said, "Don't eat any of the meat balls—we need all of them for the company this evening."

How did she know that I was even thinking about it? Maybe she had the same temptation. No issue; I was busy with my chores.

A few minutes later she followed with, "Okay, one is enough, don't eat any more. We need them for tonight." I hadn't even been in the kitchen, so I retorted, "I heard you the first time." There was a muffled comment I didn't hear, and we both went about our work, she with her laundry downstairs and I with the vacuuming.

Five minutes later found the Queen pulling the plug on my vacuum as she proceeded to lay into me about the consequences of my taking the food right out of the mouths of our guests. I had no clue what she was talking about and for a moment could not even give a good answer except that I hadn't had a single meatball. I could tell I wasn't believed. To say she was furious was an understatement. I was about to make some romantic remark about how sexy she looked with flames darting out of her ears but thought better of it. My experience is that times like this are not appropriate for sexy remarks. Go figure.

Then she used a line that has become a mainstay of our marriage. The words are different depending on what item you are talking about, but the sentiment is always the same. "So I suppose the meatball bandit came in and stole half of our meatballs and then left."

You could cut the sarcasm with a knife, but I had to admit she had a point. At that time, I had not started my career in food science, but even I knew that meatballs don't evaporate. It looked like I was caught red-handed doing something I never did in the first place. There was no way that pleading innocence was going to get me anywhere.

She wanted to make sure I knew the severity of my crime, so she requested that I follow her into the kitchen. I actually think she grabbed me and dragged me, but she remembers this part being less violent. As we entered the kitchen, her still lecturing me about how I was going to have to drive to the store for more chop meat, the culprit was discovered. We saw our three-month-old Labrador-Shepherd mix on top of the counter next to the stove in the act of devouring the remaining meatballs.

I wasn't sure if relief for being vindicated or pure laughter would be the appropriate response. I found out from the Queen that neither was correct. Rage was the only response the Queen had an interest in. She may have made good meatballs, but she was still Irish in the temper category.

The puppy, named Pepper, instinctively knew something was wrong. I think the shrieking gave that away. Pepper darted for the other side of the kitchen. The Queen caught the poor mutt near the basement steps, grabbed her by the scuff of the neck, and threw her down the stairs. I never realized that puppies bounce so well.

I was off to the store for more chop meat, onions, etc, while Pepper was in the doghouse. Funny thing about dogs: They never forget an experience like that. Pepper was always a little leery about eating meat even if we put it in her dish. Does the name Pavlov ring a bell?

Gary Vageri: *Ya know, the comic strip guy*

I have a very close friend whom I have known since the mid-1970s: July 19, 1976, to be exact. Of all the friends I have made as an adult, he is my closest. He has helped me in tough times, and, hopefully, I have helped him along the way. We started as young engineers at the same company a week apart. At that time, we even looked alike: two mustachioed young chemical engineers from the New York area with large builds working in the same department. His name is Gary, mine Gerry. Everyone got us confused.

Beside the physical, Gary and I are so alike it is scary. We both have two daughters: Both have Irish-American wives who are good at sports, and both of our fathers were named Arthur. Could he be my brother? Could he be me?

One day someone called the factory wanting to speak to either one of us. The person said, "I'll speak to Gary or Gerry." Since he was speaking in a New York accent, the receptionist understood him to say "Gary Vageri" and told the caller, "No one by that name works here."

But Gary's name is not Vageri. It's Larson. He has the same name as the comic strip writer who became famous for "The Far Side" series. This has led to interesting situations. He has been asked a number of times, "Are you the real Gary Larson?" to which he responds "Yes." His name is Gary Larson and he is real. Since he is actually older than the "Far Side" Gary Larson, you could say he is "more real" than the guy who did the comic strip.

Once a gate attendant on an airline ran aboard the plane just before they closed the door and asked, "Are you Gary Larson?" He said yes, thinking she was asking for some airline reason, but when she presented him with the comic book to sign, he calmly signed it. Hey, she can honestly state that Gary Larson signed her book.

One of the traits that I admire in this friend is that he never sweats the small stuff. He doesn't even sweat the big stuff. He has as even a keel as anyone I know. Okay, on the golf course once I saw him get upset—once. I was also there for his eagle. Yes, he was excited, but had it been me who sank a 180-yard five iron, I would have sought out CNN and held a press conference. He acted as if it happened every day.

He treats everything calmly. I remember helping him put up his daughters' swing set in their back yard in 1976. Tracy, who was three, was "helping" us, and I, not having kids yet, thought it would be good idea for her to hold some nuts and bolts while I was fitting a piece in. Gary calmly looked over and said, "You know you will never see those nuts and bolts again." Had it been me I would have flown across the yard and grabbed them from her hand.

I have shared much with my friend Gary. We climbed our first Alp together. We tried Paul Newman's "stick your face in ice water to keep young" strategy together. We did the forty-five-holes-in-one-day golf marathon together.

We even started our great American novel together. He wrote one chapter and I wrote the next, then we would alternate. This started in

1981, and since we have five chapters completed in twenty-eight years, I estimate we will be done in the year 2145. One of the reasons we have stalled a little is the fact that he tends to kill off my characters in his chapters. The good news is, if we win the Nobel Prize for literature in 2146, the prize should be over 100 million dollars by then. I can't wait!

Grumpy

My dad died at fifty-five, when I was twenty-four. He was a gentle, quiet man, and I often wonder what our relationship would have been had he lived longer. I did have a surrogate in a way, my father-in-law.

Because I meet my wife when I was fifteen, I have known my father-in-law for a long time. At first, through the eyes of a teenager dating his daughter, I was intimidated by the guy. Later I came to consider him as a second father. It certainly helped that he and my dad got along well. When he became a grandfather, wow, what a softy this guy became. How could I have ever feared him?

I chose the title of this piece very carefully—not because he was grumpy at all, but because he pretended to be. We called him Grampy, but he had a hat with *Grumpy* on it. You know—the Disney dwarf.

The stories about Grampy are legendary in our family. A child of the Depression, he was always concerned with costs. He had a stroke while dining at an IHOP restaurant. While they were taking him to the hospital, he made sure to tell his son, "Make sure you get the senior's discount on the meal."

He was frugal enough to want to fix anything that broke; Depression children are like that. Today we just buy a new one. Back then, you repaired it. The only issue was that he often ended up with a few extra pieces after he had the item put back together.

His friends tell a story of him trying to skip out of paying a bar bill during his time in the service, but he had to go back to get his hat. The hat cost more than the bar bill, so he ended up paying for the drinks.

He was a proud New York City Irishman whose father was a cop. He and I discovered a few things together. Let's see. There was the time that we discovered Black Russians. Then there was the time we discovered Manhattans, then martinis. I personally take partial credit for him discovering wine. I am Italian, you know.

He never went overseas during the war, for a number of reasons. He ended up guarding Italian prisoners in New England. He told a story of them teaching him soccer. While he was kicking the ball, he handed his gun to one of the prisoners. I think he really didn't like Italians at all growing up. He had two kids: one married an Astorino and one a Tortorelli. He came to love both sets of in-laws. I claim that is because the Tortorelli connection happened first. Who knows what would have occurred if the Astorinos were the first in the family.

One of the funniest things that I have every witnessed occurred while drinking Italian wine with him. A friend had given them a wine decanter, quite elaborate. It looked just like a bottle of Chianti with the bottom encased in straw. It had a spout, however, coming off of the main part of the bottle about a third of the way up. Theoretically, you would hold the bottle by the neck and pour out of the spout.

On this particular occasion, he noticed that my glass was empty and asked if I wanted more wine. I said yes and he proceeded to clasp the bottle by the top and attempt to pour from the top, forgetting about the spout. The result was that the spout was emptying the bottle onto his lap while he was trying to fill my glass. No one picked up on this for a few seconds and then … well, it was the funniest thing I have ever seen. Even my mother-in-law, who should have been upset that her carpet was dripping with red wine, could not stop laughing.

My two daughters were close to Grampy and delighted in seeing him. I would often reflect on this: the man who intimidated his future son-in-law was the most loving and caring grandfather. We all can take a lesson from that. Maybe the lesson is that it is never too late to change, or maybe the lesson is to make your sons-in-law jump through hoops. I think he would voice the second idea, but deep down he was the embodiment of the first.

Toothpaste, mayonnaise, and Big Ben

When I married the Queen, a brother came along with the deal: my brother-in-law, the Queen's lone sibling. I wasn't sure how that would work. The way I looked at it, I had a lifetime of sibling rivalry to catch up on.

When my brother-in-law, Jim, and his wife, Carol, visited us in Switzerland, we put a tube of mayonnaise on the bathroom sink. In Switzerland, condiments like ketchup, mustard, and mayo come in tubes similar to toothpaste. A few minutes after he entered the bathroom, we heard him shout, "Carol, get our toothpaste! This stuff is disgusting!" Even the Queen enjoyed that one.

What really amazes me is the relationship my brother-in-law has with my wife. Jim is a partner in a law firm. He is nobody's fool, yet he is putty in his sister's hands. This really gets under Carol's skin. When the Queen decided she would stop working at the age of forty-three, I thought she could make a great living being a consultant to whomever Jim was suing at the time. There would be no contest: Jim could be winning a case handily, but when in she walked as a witness for his adversary, bingo, he would fold. Sorry to say, she didn't heed my advice—something about family unity.

The control that my wife has over her brother first manifested itself about thirty-three years ago when we were deciding what movie to see. Carol had suggested to Jim that we see *The Boys from Brazil,* and he had dismissed this rather abruptly. When his sister called a half hour later and suggested the same film, Jim thought it was the greatest idea in the world. I think it took a lot of self-control on Carol's part not to kill him right there and then.

I like my brother-in-law enough, but he can get under my skin. Let me give you an example: St Peter's Church in Zürich. What, you have never heard of it? That's funny. It's the largest clock face in Europe. I made sure I pointed this out to Jim during the tour we gave Carol and him in 1982. Jim's immediate response was "Yeah, sure. It can't be bigger than Big Ben. You must mean on the continent of Europe." I told him no, largest in all Europe. He dismissed me as an uninformed tourist. By the way, *tourist* is the worst thing you can call someone who actually lives in a country.

I didn't harbor any ill feelings about this, and, really, I forgot the comment until 2004 (twenty-two years later). Back in Zürich on a business trip, leafing through a guidebook, I saw the words jump off the page: "Largest clock face in Europe."

This time I had the Internet to prove that I was right. After a short search, I had clear proof that St Peter's beats Big Ben by almost Jim's own height.[2] I wasn't sure what effect my triumphant e-mail would have on him. I would have been happy with a "Wow, I guess you were right," or "Really, I was wrong, wasn't I?" or, even better, "Forgive me, for I am an idiot for ever doubting you. I guess you were right all those years ago. I wonder what other numerous things you have been right about over this long time." I like the last response. I hoped he would use it.

The response I actually got was not exactly like that. It was more, "What are you talking about?" "I don't remember any of that," and finally, the worst of all, "If you still remember that after all these years, you should get a life."

I can categorically state that I am now cured of the in-law sibling rivalry thing. But this got me thinking. If he forgot about the Big Ben thing, maybe he forgot about everything that happened during his trip to Switzerland. Just in case, last month I brought back a nice, large tube of Swiss mayonnaise.

---

2   St Peter's is 28 ft, 6 in. in diameter versus Big Ben at 23 ft, 0 in.

3. CH, UK,[3] and the tower of Babel revisited

In 1981, our small family immigrated to a village in the German-speaking part of Switzerland. Two years later, we moved to the French-speaking part. A year after that, we moved to the UK (where I think they speak English). I'm not sure what we expected, but it was culturally and linguistically clear that this wasn't the Bronx any longer!

---

3   CH: The international abbreviation for Switzerland = Confederation Helvetica
     UK: The international abbreviation for the United Kingdom of Great Britain
     and Northern Ireland, not to be confused with the University of Kentucky

The other side

In 1981, our young family moved to Switzerland. The whole thing sounds daring, but at the time we were too naïve to really understand what we were getting into. We developed into a close-knit family unit, not to mention the move generated some great family folklore. It is a part of our lives that we cherish.

The intention was that we spend two years in the German-speaking part of Switzerland and then return to our raised ranch in Connecticut in time for our oldest princess, Beth, to begin kindergarten. However, after additional stints in the French-speaking part of Switzerland, the UK, and then Canada, we finally got back to the United States in time for my youngest princess, Lynne, to attend college. Couple this with the many visits we made to my family's town in northern Italy, and we have had an amazing time. Overall, we spent sixteen years living outside of the USA. Along the way, we picked up some language skills, a lot of memorabilia, some great customs, and even two sons-in-law.

We were a young family going through things that a stateside young family does: trying to figure out how to make ends meet at the end of the month, shopping for essentials, and trying to fit in vacations. Granted, we had the choice of jumping in a car and driving to Venice for the weekend instead of Cape Cod, but everything else seemed the same.

Right from the start, we realized things would be different. As we were planning our move, my company's Swiss Human Resources group contacted us, saying that they found us an apartment. Apartments in that part of Switzerland at that time were hard to get, so having one ahead of time would really help. They gave us the dimensions of the rooms and a description that read in part, "first-floor apartment in a farmhouse." It sounded great, so we took it.

The first surprise when we actually got there was that although the farmhouse was at the main crossroads of the village, it was still a farmhouse. These old Swiss villages have homes with connected barns. Most were in town, and the farmers' fields were not adjacent to their homes but out of town. This is a throwback to hundreds of years ago when the populace huddled together in the town for protection, with the fields on the outskirts.

The second surprise was that the European ground floor is what we call the first floor, and the first floor is what we would call the second floor. So we had an apartment on the second floor of a farmhouse in the middle of the village. This was fine by us. In fact, it was a great set-up because we were near the little grocery store and the milk cooperative.

Our first months in Switzerland were a constant education in new and different ways to look at things. The Swiss compulsion for both cleanliness and maximum utilization of all resources was and still is evident all around the country. A good example is something I like to call "the neat forests."

As I write this piece, I am looking out my home office window at the woods behind my house in Solon, Ohio. I own half of these woods, while my neighbor owns the other half. Since it is early spring and no leaves impede my view, I can easily see seven or eight downed trees. Some of these have been down for as long as we have owned the home; others came down more recently. Numerous branches and limbs have fallen to the forest floor. Many of these have started to decay back into the soil. This is a typical American forest.

Not so in Switzerland. I do not think there is a law against messy forests, but all Swiss forests that are anywhere near inhabited areas are neat. By the way, since it is a small country, "anywhere near inhabited areas" includes about 99.5 percent of Switzerland.

We would kid that this was a result of the Swiss compulsion for organization and cleanliness, but, in fact, it represents their compulsion that they use all resources to the maximum. They don't waste anything. Felled trees and limbs, whether brought down by a storm, lightning, or any other reason, are wood that can be used. It is to be cut to a standard length, stacked in a neat stack, and carted, when appropriate, to a location where it can be used. Many times on our hikes, we would see stacks of wood in the middle of neat forests. North America is a disposable society. We could learn a lot from the Swiss.

After the Swiss experience, we moved to the UK. We settled in England, to be exact: in the town of Marlow in South Buckinghamshire, to be even more exact. This community is forty-five minutes west of central London when there is no traffic, which is never.

We knew from the outset that our language skills would be tested. Upon arriving at Heathrow that April afternoon in 1984, the immigration officer questioned us on the middle names of the princesses. We had given them my wife's maiden name, Ruddy, as middle names. We told him this, and he turned to a colleague and said, "This couple has two ruddy kids." They both fell over laughing. *Ruddy* is a mild expletive in the UK.

We had a great time on the other side of the pond. It was a real experience for two kids from the Bronx, who always assumed we would live in the New York Metropolitan area forever. I treasure it for the experience Sue and I had, but also for its affect on the next generation. Of the thirty-nine years of schooling that our two princesses went through, only four were spent in the United States: the four years Lynne spent at Purdue University.

The Altikon years

When we first arrived in Switzerland, we stayed in a hotel, awaiting the arrival of our belongings, which had been shipped down the Rhine. Sue and I haven't been on a Rhine cruise, but our couch has.

After the hotel stay, we set up home in the small village of Altikon. Settling in was a real treat, like learning a completely new way of life in about two days, or at least it seemed like it.

I have had friends who have done overseas stints, and some commented on how little effort it was to fit in to the other culture. Upon speaking with them, I often realize that they lived in a little ex-pat ghetto, where most of their friends were also expatriated and most were English-speakers. Many such people spend a lot of time trying to figure out how they can live like Americans in another land. We were very fortunate to live "on the economy," as military folks call it. We lived with the Swiss, as the Swiss. Looking back, this was a fantastic choice. However, at any given time between 1981 and 1985, you could have easily convinced us that we had made a big mistake.

Beth, my oldest, was two months shy of her fourth birthday when we moved. She started kindergarten (a German word, by the way) with nine other kids and a teacher, none of whom spoke a word of English. Actually, that is an exaggeration. They all knew the words to "Happy

Birthday" in English. Beth became fluent in Swiss-German kidspeak in no time: small vocabulary, but unaccented and fluent.

The town had a Reformed church, but the Catholic church was a fifteen-minute drive away. We did not attend church much in those days. Had there been English mass, we might have, but to get to that we had to drive an hour to Zürich proper.

When we checked in with the town hall, as all foreigners must do, we did claim we were Catholic when asked. We then found out that Catholics pay higher taxes. The two main churches in Kanton Zürich are Catholic and Reformed. Both are funded by a church tax that is added to your income tax. The Catholic taxes at that time had higher rates. We asked how many other families were Catholic in Altikon. They said one other, and they had six kids. Sue commented, "We're not that Catholic." We still had to pay the taxes, though.

The time we spent in this small town in a German-speaking part of this alpine country is among the most precious we have had in our family's life. There were no distractions, like English TV, that diverted out attention away from the family. We were our own little unit, and we were dependent on each other. Maybe we saw this as a bit of a trial at the time, but in hindsight, it was a blessing we relish to this day. It's like the young couple who later in life remember their first apartment as a mansion, when in fact it was a third the size of where they live now. I wouldn't change the "Altikon years" for the world.

Real Swiss buttons… "Echte Schweizer Knöpfli"

When we moved to Switzerland, I was a young, wet-behind-the-ears chemical engineer with a background in food science. The first project I was assigned was to improve the quality and cost of the *knöpfli* that was produced at the local factory.

Knöpfli is a Swiss German word that literally translated means "small buttons." The term describes a Swiss dumpling, a side dish with many Swiss meals. It is similar in a way to German spetzels.

Traditionally the product is made in the home from fresh dough that resembles North American pancake batter. The batter is put into a sieve with holes about three-eighths of an inch in diameter, and the batter drips into boiling water, where it cooks rather quickly. The resulting knöpfli are small dumplings that can later be fried or eaten with sauces.

In the hustle and bustle of 1980s Switzerland, many people did not have the time to cook knöpfli from scratch. Hence the need for the factory-made, dehydrated variety that I was working on. It was probably akin to the first dried pasta produced in Italy after the war. Fresh-made is good, but a shelf-stable pasta that you could keep in the cupboard and cook whenever you wanted was a great idea. These ready-made knöpfli had been on the market before I arrived, but our intent was to improve the quality of the product; making it more like homemade.

So there I was, a newly immigrated American engineer, charged with the job of improving the quality of a traditional Swiss dish. You would think that this was a recipe for disaster.

After three months of trials in both the pilot plant and the factory, plus numerous equipment and recipe modifications, we achieved what we were looking for: a shelf-stable knöpfli that was much closer to the texture and flavor of the fresh-made variety. The claim on the box was "Ecther Schweizer Knöpfli"—*Real Swiss Knöpfli*.

Looking at our project gives you a good idea about how Swiss society works. I cannot disclose the recipe for the product, but here are the "ingredients" that went into the project.

To produce "Real Swiss Knöpfli," do the following: Import one project leader from the United States (me). Hire three shifts of trained factory workers, all of whom were immigrants from Yugoslavia. Make the batter from hard wheat flour produced in Canada and eggs imported from Poland. Season the batter with nutmeg, grown on a Caribbean island. Then process through various pieces of pasta equipment made in Italy.

One might ask, so what was so "real Swiss" about our knöpfli? The answer is simple: the water. Ah, the Swiss! How else could a country be so famous for its chocolate and not have one indigenous cocoa plant?

Improve your English—in Switzerland

Before the family moved to the German-speaking part of Switzerland, we had German lessons—not the princesses, of course, who were two and four years old, but the adults. We were told that the kids would pick up German rather quickly. That is exactly what happened with the four-year-old, who started kindergarten soon after we arrived. The two-year-old ended up speaking English with a German accent because she heard a lot of German speakers use English. Since she had bangs and a German accent, I once referred to her as Little Adolph. The Queen was not impressed.

We adults did okay, mostly because we choose to live in a small village. As it turned out, the village had no English speakers except for us. At work, I was the only native English speaker at the site. The official language at work was English, and all the project leaders and management spoke English pretty well, but none were native speakers. This resulted in an odd phenomenon: My English improved while I lived in a non-English-speaking country.

At the onset, most of the project leaders came to me individually and asked that we speak only English, since they needed to improve their language skills. This was not much of a chore for me, as my German was quite terrible. As time progressed, however, it became clear that if I spoke in my typical New York cadence with my normal Bronxisms, they were not going to understand me in English either. I ended up slowing down and taking the time and effort to pronounce the words correctly.

I can recall chatting with a colleague in English one Friday. He had asked what we were going to do on the weekend. We had planned to take a ride into the mountains to see the scenery. My answer was in typical Bronxese. "We wanna go to Lichtenstein this weekend," I stated. He wore that dumbfounded look, the one when you know they have not a clue about what you just said. He then asked, "What does 'wanna' mean?" I explained that it means "want to," but in New York, we often shorten the words. Of course, a native English speaker, even one from Scotland or New Zealand, would have understood enough through the usage to grasp the meaning, but English was this gentleman's third language.

Similar things happened with words like *member* for *remember*, as in "'Member when we did the last consumer test?" Another example would be *kinda* for *kind of*, as in "I'm kinda hungry." As a result, I knew I had to speak better English there.

After a few months of speaking more slowly and being very deliberate with my pronunciation, I ran into a colleague who was visiting from the U.S. company. Near the end of our conversation, he asked if I had had a stroke or some similar problem, because I was speaking so slowly.

I must state in defense of all New Yorkers that we are not the only ones who take short cuts in English. The best way to tell if someone is not from Ontario is ask him/her to say "Toronto." An Ontario native pronounces their biggest city similar to the capital of Albania, Tirana. If you hear a hard second *t*, you are talking to a non-Canadian.

Besides slowing down and being vigilant about pronunciation, I discovered that my word usage also changed. This resulted from the fact that most Swiss learn their English in schools that teach the Queen's English, not the President's kind. When all your associates are speaking one way, you tend to pick up their word usage without even realizing it. Once, while I was on home leave in the United States, I asked my brother-in-law from Long Island how long a certain "journey" would be by car. He gave me a look and answered, "About an hour and a half, but here we call it a trip."

After Switzerland, we spent two years in England. Although the UK experience certainly had a linguistic effect, the best English I ever spoken was in Switzerland. That is funny, because now I speak Swiss German with a Bronx accent ... go figure.

A good fahrt ... and a douche

After reading the title of this piece, you'd think I can't spell and that I am very rude indeed.

The word *fahrt* (pronounced exactly like the English would *fart*) is the root of many a German saying that involves driving. *fahren* is the German verb that means to drive, while *die Fahrt* is the noun for a drive.

In German, one can also put two words together to make a third. For example: an exit from the Autobahn is an *Ausfahrt*, meaning driving out (aus = out). A drive in the countryside would be simply a Fahrt.

Even though I knew this, it still took me by surprise the first time a colleague wished me a good drive with a hearty "Gute Farht." I wondered what he knew about my bowels that I didn't.

In a similar manner, the Swiss have an interesting way of identifying the specials in shops. The word *hit* is often used. If it is a good price, they often use the phrase *price hit*, in German written *Preishit*. Of the daily special, they say "hit of the day," in German "Tageshit. If you break the syllables before the *s*, it does make for interesting reading in English.

The oddest thing, however, is to hear a foreign word in an English sentence. The coup de resistance is the French or German word for *shower*. When used in a French sentence, it seems very natural. However, when thrown into an English sentence, it can raise an eyebrow or two.

I was once asked when checking into a hotel if I wanted a room with a shower. They had rooms with showers and some with baths. Sensing from my accent that I was an English speaker, the front desk lady spoke partly in French and partly in English. I wonder if she understood why I laughed so hard when she asked, "Do you want a room and a douche?"

They never ask that at the Holiday Inn in Connecticut.

Boiling clothes and pounds of cheese

Now, let's talk about washing white clothes—the white wash, my favorite of all washes. In our Ohio home, white wash is the only one we do on the hot setting. We use cold for everything else. I'm not even sure if the warm setting on our washing machine is functional. I'll have to try it next time.

We use the hot setting for white wash and we add bleach, which we buy in gallon jugs, like most families in North America. I am a purist and prefer the unscented bleach best, and I only buy the leading brand. Sue is more pragmatic and buys whatever is on sale.

I have no market data, but I'm sure the guys at Proctor & Gamble could quote you statistics on how "normal" our washing routine is. I bet it's pretty normal for North America. The key phrase is "for North America."

On our first grocery shopping trip in Switzerland in 1981, we wanted to buy bleach. We were informed by a puzzled-looking neighbor that it is called Javel Wasser and that it would be available at a drug store in a very small bottle. We thought this was funny, but hey, it was Switzerland. The neighbor asked why we wanted it, and when we explained that it was to wash clothes, she thought it was a joke.

In Switzerland, as in most of Europe, bleach is not used in home laundries. Instead you wash your clothes on the hot setting. Well, we use the hot setting in North America, but their hot setting is around 205° F. That is slightly below the boiling point of water, by the way. So, in a way, our hot setting "ain't so hot."

Like much of Europe, only cold water is plumbed into the washing machines in Switzerland. The washing machine heats the water itself. A white wash in Switzerland takes between two and two and a half hours. But let me tell you, the clothes are clean, very clean. Try boiling your underwear in your spaghetti pot one day. If you do, I guarantee two things: Your underwear will be clean, and I will not come to your house for spaghetti.

One day in 1982 Sue washed Lynne's ski jacket on the hot setting. To get some idea of how it ended up, consider what would happen if a synthetic fiber garment were boiled on top of the stove for two hours. It is one of the times that I actually thought Sue was going to break down and cry. Funny how these things make an impact.

Now to the pounds of cheese part...

Since our small Swiss village of Altikon was a farming community, we had a Milch Zentral. This was where the local farmers took their bulk milk twice a day. While the Zentral was open, accepting milk, the store attached to it was also open. In this store, you could buy fresh milk, direct from the cows that day. We had a small aluminum milk can that held about two liters. It had a handle and a little cover. Many Swiss believed that this is the only way to have milk, right from the cow. We asked our physician if this was safe, and he informed us that there had not been a breakout of tuberculosis in ten years. I had no idea that TB came from unpasteurized milk. You learn something every day.

You could also buy cheese at the Milch Zentral. The cheese was not made in our town, but the farmers were part of the same cooperative as the cheese producers, so the cheese was a good deal. The only issue was that we knew nothing about Swiss cheeses. There are literally scores of different cheeses made in Switzerland. Most take their name from the regions in which they are made. Each region is quite proud of their cheese. They are all different from each other.

The one that North Americans know the best is Emmenthal. We know it by its American name, Swiss cheese, the one with the holes. Other main varieties are Appenzeller, Gruyere, Tête du Moine, and Tilsiter. We used to have a cheese map of Switzerland that showed about ninety types.

It was my job to take the kids to the Milch Zentral between 5:30 and 6:30 PM every day. It was about 100 yards from our back door. We would get a can of milk, still warm from the cows, and then ask for some cheese. My first goal was to get to know all the major types. This being a small shop, it had only about fifteen types of cheese. We had decided that we would buy two hundred grams (a little less than half a pound) of a different cheese each day. Great, nothing could be simpler.

Fresh from my German lessons in the United States, I was trying to speak the high German I had learned. The locals were Swiss-German speakers.

The first day after the girls and I got back, Sue commented that it was a bit more than she had expected. Indeed, it looked more like a full pound. Because that day we had chosen an aged Appenzeller, a rather potent cheese, the fridge stank for a few days.

During our next trip to the Zentral, again the quantity seemed to be more than I had requested, but at least it was a variety we liked. It went quickly, without the resultant smelly fridge. Since the Milch Zentral frau had to estimate each cut of the large cheese rounds, the amount was always an approximation. You actually paid for the exact amount when it was weighed after the cut. It was then that I started to notice that she was giving me slightly over three hundred grams each time, not the two hundred grams I had requested.

I assumed she was just trying to increase her sales, until I actually mentioned that it was too much. She looked at me and said in German, "But you wanted three hundred grams." I said no, I wanted two hundred grams and held out two fingers—the index finger and the middle finger, like the victory sign. She said, "Yes, three hundred grams," and she held out the same two fingers plus her thumb. It was then that I realized that throughout most of Europe they use the thumb to count. So all along, when I held up two fingers, she had assumed that my thumb was also in the counting equation, making my request three hundred grams instead of two.

To make matters worse, the word for two in Swiss German is nothing like the world for two in high German, so we were both totally confused.

Once I understood the thumb-counting rule and the language, we were never overstocked with cheese again. Our fridge smelled better as well.

The Swiss have a different name for every place

When you travel to another country, you are made aware of the language that separates you from the local culture at every turn. Bread, milk, cheese: Everything has its own word. There was a comedy routine in the '80s where the punch line was "The French have a different word for everything." What we didn't expect was a different name for places as well.

One of the first things we needed to do there was buy a car. The car companies are the same as in the United States, but the models differ, so it was a little like starting from scratch. A colleague suggested that I go to the Swiss National Car Show, which happened to be starting the following week in a place called Genf. I could see all the cars available in Switzerland under one roof. This was a great idea. This conversation occurred in German, by the way.

I asked how far Genf was. He informed me that it was about a three-hour drive, or I could take the train. "In which direction is Genf?" I asked.

He explained the route to me. Funny, it sounded like it was in the direction of Geneva. So I asked, "Is it near Geneva?"

Again came the dumbfounded look that tells you immediately that you have said something incomprehensible to someone.

His answer, "Genf is Geneva. Genf is how you say Geneva in German."

Well, isn't that a pip! They even renamed the cities.

I knew that Geneva with an *a* is English, and Geneve with an *e* is French; at least the pronunciation is close, but *Genf*?

This gets even more complicated; there are often four names for Swiss cities because there are four national languages. Even more interesting, there are four names for the country:

Switzerland = Schweiz (G), Suisse (F), Svizzera (I), and Svizra (Romansch)

On maps, the name that is printed for a particular city is the one used by most of the inhabitants. Therefore, Zurich appears on Swiss maps as *Zürich*, the German version, as most of the inhabitants speak German, not as *Zurigo*, the Italian name.

Well, we never got to Genf to the car show. We bought a Honda Quintet, a model not available in the United States at the time—unless the Americans called it by a different name.

The conquest of Pointe des Vouasson

When one thinks of Switzerland, one thinks of chocolate, cheese, and mountains. Moving to Switzerland in the early 1980s gave our friends a chance to visit Europe and use our place as a home base during their travels.

My friends enjoyed mountain hiking. Actually, my men friends thought this a great idea, while our spouses and kids thought we were a bit crazy. In two cases, cable cars went to the top of the mountains we climbed, so we could have saved ourselves some aching muscles had we joined our families in the cable cars. We, of course, are manly men, so we had to conquer the mountains ourselves.

One problem with manly men is that they always want to do more than other manly men do. Hence, of the three friends who came to Switzerland to climb, each had to go higher than the previous visitor.

The first fellow who came was Gary. We climbed a mountain in eastern Switzerland named Säntis, 2502 m (6,732 ft). Although not recommended for people who don't like heights, it is a simple, three-and-a-half hour afternoon climb, but very interesting, especially as the last two hundred or so feet goes straight up ladders in the side of the rock face. There is a small snowfield section, but no glaciers or crevasses were on our route. All the rest is switchbacks. Our ascent was without any issue, except for the last section, when a wind came up and the temperature dropped by thirty degrees. We had planned for this and had gloves in our packs.

This was one of the mountains with a cable car, and ladies in high heels and Japanese tourists greeted us at the summit. Our families joined us a little later, and we enjoyed a nice late-day lunch in the restaurant close to the summit. I can't speak for Gary, but I was insulted by these "tourists" coming onto my mountain. Hey, I climbed it. All they did was pay twenty francs and take a ride on a subway car on a string. I guess I had become a mountaineering snob.

Well, my snobbery wore off when I realized that we were going to take the cable car down, as it was too late in the day to climb down. But my snobbery emerged again when I made sure the guy behind me in the line knew that I climbed up by loudly ordering my one-way ticket. Yeah, I am a mountaineering snob.

The next friend who came to visit, Rod, wanted to go higher, so we went to the top of the Eggishorn, at a height of 2,927 m (9,602 ft). Again, this was a half-day climb, and we came down via the cable car. This was an easier climb but in some ways more enjoyable, as the view was incredible. We were able to see all the major mountains of Switzerland.

Now all this was fine. At no time did I actually fear for my life during these treks. They were relaxing and strenuous but never dangerous. Then came the "Pratt man": Jim Pratt, to be exact. He had to go higher than either of the other two. But where?

By this time, we had moved to the French-speaking part of Switzerland, and I didn't know which mountains would be climbable by mere novices. I went to visit the person in charge of the mountaineering club at our company. He had an immediate answer: Pointe des Vouasson, 3,490 m (11,413 ft). We would not need crampons or ropes, just good shoes for this gentle two-day climb. The two-day part should have been my first clue.

To Jim's delight, this was to be the most arduous climb to date, with no cable car to take us back down. It was also to be the highest. The ascent would be made over a two-day period. This found us overnighting in an Alpine hut at 2,821 m (9,225 ft)

This happened during the time I was keeping a journal. The actual climb takes up about thirty pages in a special journal that I started for the Pratts' visit. The journal had a *Return of the Jedi* cover and was entitled "My Jedi Journal… A special diary for Jedi Knights in Training." What could be more appropriate?

We started out (Base Camp 1) in a little town below the mountain in the early afternoon. Very soon we were above the tree line on a beautiful day. As we gained altitude, breathing became harder. I was surprised at this because we were still below 10,000 feet. Late in the afternoon, we arrived at the Alpine cabin that was run by two ladies. The place is called Cabane des Aiguilles Rouges (Cabin of the Red Needle Peak).

This refuge was a welcome sight. It gave us a chance to rest, have some food that we had brought along, and drink some hot bouillon, which is about all you can buy at the cabin. This cabin is situated on top of a sheer cliff that falls off about 1,200 feet. We had come up on switchbacks around the rear of the wall. The scenery was breathtaking.

While we were enjoying the sunset, two interesting things happened. The first entailed us being introduced to the toilet there. It is of course a good idea to get rid of any human waste that in generated. No one wants this stuff just lying around. Here is the dilemma: Alps are made of rock, solid rock, so septic tanks don't really work. What to do? Anyone who thinks about mountains knows two things. They are high, and the easiest direction to go when you are high up is down.

The outhouse consisted of two small buildings built on a platform over the sheer precipice. Once you went in and opened the cover, there was nothing between you and the ground, almost a quarter of a mile down. Now we realized why the hiking trail did not go through this area. An added attraction was that once you sat down, there was no light. The only light came up through the hole that you were covering by sitting down.

The second interesting thing that happened that evening occurred when we were discussing our plans with the lady who ran the cabin. First, she wanted to know which peak we were heading for. There are a number you can reach from this cabin. After we told her, she informed us that we would be put in the same dorm room as the other thirteen people heading for Pointe des Vouasson. We were all to be awakened at a 5:30 so we could be off the glacier before it was too warm and the ice melted.

I think that is what she said. All I heard was the word *glacier*. 1983 had been a warm year, and there seemed to be weekly stories of climbers falling into crevasses with soft, melting ice. In fact, the Queen had made us promise that we would not traverse any glaciers. A snowfield was okay, but no glaciers.

The lady went on to ask if we had crampons. I looked at Jim, and he looked at me. Sensing we did not have any, she added, "You really don't need them anyway." That was easy for her to say. She wasn't going to be featured in the Lausanne paper the next day in the article entitled, "Two Americans Lost on Glacier."

The next question should have been the showstopper. "Where are your ropes?" she inquired. Flashback to the head of the mountaineering club saying, "No ropes, no crampons required. Just a good pair of shoes."

"What are the ropes for?" Jim asked.

The answer was something neither of us wanted to hear. "If one of you falls in a crevasse, the other pulls him out," she answered.

Jim accepted that answer. I wanted to ask, "What would stop the first one from pulling the second into the crevasse behind him?" but I didn't. The answer involves sinking an ice axe into the snow and wrapping the rope around it. This was a moot point, since neither one of us had an ice axe.

At that time, I weighed about two hundred pounds, and Jim must have been about a hundred and forty. If I went into the crevasse, I thought we were both going in. But if he went in, we might have a chance. Only after we were safely off the mountain did I tell him of my intention to cut the rope if he fell in first. Those Swiss Army knives could come in handy.

She did suggest we take one of her ropes. This was reassuring. No true Swiss would lend a rope to someone they thought would leave it under their dead body at the bottom of a crevasse. What a waste of rope that would be. This woman obviously felt we were in no danger.

The nice rope-lending lady casually mentioned that the group ahead of us, thirteen strong, had a guide with a glacier-testing pole. He would check the ice, and the team would be following in his footsteps. She suggested that we follow behind them. In my mind I was paraphrasing a famous expression: "Lead, follow, or fall in a crevasse." We would gladly follow.

We decided that we would stick as close to the group ahead of us as possible. She supported that theme by informing us that part of this group, made up of both men and women, would be sleeping in the same dorm room as we would be. New headline: "Americans Fall in Crevasse After Spending Night with Swiss Female Mountain Climbers." I wouldn't have to worry about the fall; the Queen would kill me.

I slept amazingly well in our co-ed dorm room. I think it was the altitude. They did wake us up at 5:30, with the intent that we get moving by 6:30. We all slept in our clothes. One woman in the bunk across from me changed her shirt before we headed off. Even in the dark, I could see her in her bra. For an American in 1983, a woman changing in front of men was still a novelty. She didn't catch me looking at her. If I died in a crevasse that day, how was I going to explain my naughty peek to Saint Peter, I wondered.

At 6:20, Jim and I headed off before the group of thirteen. We weren't going onto the glacier before they did, but we certainly didn't want them to get ahead of us too far. At 7:25, we arrived at the glacier, with the group behind us. We all stopped and tied ourselves together. They had three climbers per rope, except the lead who had four. We had only two. The rope that the nice lady from the cabin lent us was in fact long enough to tie together an entire regiment of Alpine military climbers. We doubled it and then doubled it again so we had four ropes running between us. It would be very difficult for me to cut through if Jim fell in.

We snaked around what seemed to be numerous crevasses for almost two hours before we reached the summit. The closest we got to the mouth of a crevasse was about fifteen feet. The problem was that this crevasse was down the glacier from us, so if one of us slipped, he would slide down the glacier into the crevasse. This was nerve-racking, to say the least.

At 9:33, we summitted Pointe des Vouasson. The glacier ended about two hundred meters from the summit. The summit itself was plain loose rock and no issue at all. What a difference from the other mountains I had climbed with Gary and Rod. They had little cities at their summits. This one was miles from any civilization.

After fifteen minutes on the peak, during which we rehydrated and carbed up, we were ready for the descent. Luckily, we followed the exact route down without stops. At 11:03, we were down off the glacier. It was one of the five times in my life that I was so elated that my skin tingled.

The rest of the day was laborious and fun at the same time—the type of fun you can only enjoy when some nerve-racking task has just ended. We drank from an alpine stream; we crossed a meadow and a cow charged at us (probably a bull, but I'm a city guy and I think it is rude to look at an animal's privates, so I am still not sure). Finally, we had a great bowl of pea soup at a restaurant in the valley.

Fast forward twenty-two years.

The Pratts called a few months ago. It seems one of their sons was to be in Ohio as manager of his college's women's volleyball team. Talk about a great job. We made arrangements to see him while he was here. It was great catching up on old times. We last saw him some seven years ago.

During our visit I happened to mention the conquest of Pointe des Vouasson. I wondered if his father had ever mentioned it to him, since he wasn't even born at the time. Well, indeed it had gone down in Pratt family folklore.

Jim's son did not recall it as the days during which his father and a friend conquered fear and strove together to the top of some Alp. Nor is it remembered for the daring of those two young climbers who attempted this feat with a borrowed rope, without crampons or an ice axe. It is remembered as the day when his father and a friend had to poop off a cliff. Ah, youth. Maybe they have the right idea.

A different attitude

We moved to the UK a few months before the coal miners' strike of 1984 and 1985. We moved out eighteen months later, a little after it ended. I don't even know if a miners' strike in the United States would be noticed by most people, but in the UK, in the mid-eighties, it was a devastating and tumultuous event that affected the entire country.

The mines were run by the government. Many of the mines were too costly to run. The coal they produced was more expensive than the price it could raise on the open market. The government decided to shut down some of the mines. The union went on strike, closing all mines in the country to protest the government policies.

Whether or not you are pro-union or anti-union doesn't really matter for this tale. I will not try to defend one position or the other. I'm sure a Yankee living in the UK could not even begin to understand the complexities of the issues back then, and time has made the politics even more remote to me now.

No, this little story is about a personal attitude that surprised me so much I remember it still. I saw this during a human-interest story on Channel Four, one of the TV stations in Brittan then. The point was to show the impact of the mine closures on families. I can still see the television as if it were yesterday.

The reporter was interviewing a miner somewhere in the Midlands, in a town in which the mine was scheduled to close. The miner was being interviewed in his living room while his five-year-old son played on the floor next to him. There were some questions, some answers, and a hearty thank you to his miner brethren who were on the picket line trying to save his job.

Then came the comment that has stuck with me for twenty-five years. The miner said, "My grandfather worked in this mine. My father worked in this mine. I work in this mine. If they close it down, what is my son going to do?" During the last phrase, the camera panned to the innocent child playing at his father's feet.

He didn't say, "Where is the next generation of miners going to work?" No. He said, "Where is my son going to work?" It was personal. This was about his family. It was clear that his son would not have a mine to work in if the government got their way. However, that was the point that shocked me, that this father-miner would be so accepting of his son's lot in life. I chalked it up at the time to a British "accept your position in society" attitude.

My parents and their parents always wanted the next generation to do better than they did. In my naiveté, I had assumed that everyone in the world thought that way. In my mind, the father-miner should have said, "My grandfather worked in this mine. My father worked in this mine. I work in this mine, and I'll be damned if my son is going to go down into the hole when he grows up!"

Members of my wife's family were originally coal miners. They emigrated from Ireland to Pennsylvania way back in the potato famine days. If it weren't for a new fangled thing called a subway that was being built in New York City and the resultant need for men who knew how to handle explosives, my wife's family would still be in Pennsylvania. I think that they would not have been in the Pennsylvania mines, however. Every generation would have moved forward.

My father, although not a miner, relayed the same opinion in the phrase, "Get a college education and do better than I did." He counseled me when I became of draft age: "Join the Navy. You'll get three meals a day and not have to dig fox holes in the rain like I did." He was always thinking about how the next generation could live a better life than he did.

What a difference between the attitude of this 1984 UK father-miner from that of my father. We were always looking to go further than the previous generation: not ready to accept our lot in life. I think that served us well, but I wonder what the young parents of today are thinking. Do they expect their kids will do better than they did?

Canons, biological functions, and knock-ups

A few days after we moved into the house in Marlow in South Buckinghamshire, UK, a neighbour[4] stopped by looking for Susan. She had heard that Susan was looking for the name of the local priest

---

4   In deference to my British friends, I am using the Queen's English spelling in this piece. The reader is asked also to pronounce the words in the British fashion while reading. Preferably using a Berkshire or South Bucks accent. (Berkshire itself is pronounced "Barksheer").

so we could register in the parish. I was working on my car, installing a radio, I recall, when Veronica came by. She introduced herself and said that she had the name of the local cannon.

Now I knew she was speaking English, and, in fact, I understood everything she said, but I wasn't sure what a cannon had to do with it. I explained that we were not a military family and didn't know why we would care about the local, or any other cannon.

She informed me that she was referring to a canon (the one *n* typed) who was the head of the local church. I proceeded to explain that we were Catholic and not COE (Church of England), so we wouldn't need the name of a canon. Now it was her turn to look at me as if I was crazy. She said that she knew we were Catholic, and she was giving us the number of the Catholic canon. At that moment, I should have understood that my language skills would be tested during our stay in the UK.

The move to the UK was a real professional change for me. Until this time, I had spent my career either on the technical side or on the technical marketing side. Now I was moving into technical sales: promoting natural food flavourings to food companies. I would have paid more attention to how I developed products had I known I would have to sell them one day.

Previously I had thought that sales jobs involved only buying someone lunch and telling a good joke. I do well in both circumstances, by the way, with eating lunch being a strong point. A technical sales job is much more involved than that, however. It is a lot like teaching. It came naturally to me. I enjoyed it.

It is critical to ask questions to discover what the customer's needs are. To help me remember all the details, I was equipped with a Dictaphone on which I could record the information before going into the next client. Remember, we are talking about pre-personal computer days. The Dictaphone tapes were sent to a secretary who would transcribe them, and I would get a hard copy a few days later.

The secretary who was in charge of typing all these visit reports was named Lesley. Actually, in our sales office, both secretaries were named Lesley. We differentiated them as "Lesley the Elder" and "Lesley the Younger." Lesley the Younger was part typist, part clerk.

After the first tape I sent in, Lesley the Younger suggested that I note the punctuation while recording. The combination of my Bronx accent and the cadence at which I spoke made it difficult for her to transcribe. I should say "comma" when I wanted a comma inserted. "Question mark" or "exclamation point" would be a piece of cake. If I really got into it, I could even use "colon" and maybe the very advanced "semi-colon." But for now, I thought all I needed was to mark my sentence's end with a simple "period."

The next time I was in the office, I asked if my tapes were any more transcribeable since I started adding the punctuation. Lesley the Younger had a look on her face that indicated she had an issue. After an uncomfortable moment, she said, in a rather official manner, "I guess I just have to blurt this out. In the United Kingdom, a dot at the end of a sentence is a 'full stop' A 'period' is a biological function." Apparently, both Lesleys had enjoyed playing my tape for everyone who would listen and commenting about the American's uncouth language.

They may have thought I was uncouth, but what would you think about Ian, one of my colleagues? As we were heading off to our hotel rooms after a sales dinner, he said, "I'll come by and knock you up in the morning." I'd like to see him try, I thought!

4. Cugini (the Italian cousins)

Sordid anecdotes about …
   faking it
   nuns
   the good Pope
   a telephone without a country
   a pocket book
   and 700 year old bones

Olgiate-Comasco: *Prima volta*

While living in Switzerland in 1982, I traveled to Italy to meet my mother's cousins in their small village just eight kilometers (five miles) from the Swiss border. The Queen and the princesses had gone back to the USA for a family fix, and I thought this would be the best possible time to make the venture. The name of the town is Olgiate-Comasco.

These are my mother's first cousins. There are a lot of them, since only my grandfather came to America, leaving his siblings in Olgiate. The extended families are quite large; the cousins had kids, and many of them now have kids of their own. There are a lot of cousins. Since my grandmother was actually a cousin to my grandfather, almost everyone in the town seems to be related to us.

When I wrote the cousins the letter explaining that I was coming, I wondered if they would know who I was. I assumed they, like me, had only a vague idea of who the family was on the other side of the ocean. Those concerns were soon forgotten when they met me at the border waving my wedding picture, which my grandmother had sent over eleven years earlier.

Our generation knew all the stories: how my grandfather came to the States at thirteen; that he had sisters he had never seen, since they were born after he left; that my grandmother was in fact a third cousin to my grandfather. It was all family folklore.

In 1982, none of the cousins spoke English except the fourteen-year-old daughter of my mother's first cousin. Her name is Morena, and she was just learning English in school. Once I received the letter from them saying they would be happy to see me, I started to teach myself Italian. By the time I arrived, I had completed a full six hours of Italian study. Let's not forget the two years of Latin in high school. Since translating Caesar's conquests leaves you with a basic knowledge of ancient warfare in a dead language, I was not hoping for much.

The cousins did think ahead. They had arranged for a young English-speaking woman from the village to be there for at least part of the day to act as a translator. At one point, the translator left and so did Morena, leaving me with my mother's first cousins, four women who spoke no English.

I tend to be very uncomfortable when there is silence among a group of people. I think someone should be talking at any given time. I felt very uncomfortable with all these Italians sitting around looking at me, so I decided to make conversation. In fairness to me, I am a good conversationalist in English. It seems to come naturally. Hey, I had six hours of self-taught Italian training and two years of high school Latin. How hard could small talk with my cousins be? Okay, I was still confused about the difference between *seventeen* and *seventy*, but numbers are overrated anyway.

Since I do not know anything about the three sports that these people seem to love, football (soccer), Formula 1 racing, and skiing, I had to make conversation on some other topic. Searching my mind for something that I believed we would have in common, I came up with a simple idea. We are all members of the Catholic Church. Since the word *catholic* means universal, this should be no problem.

Remember: The last thing you learn in a language is the gray areas. It is easy to talk about things in black and white, but the nuances of gray only come with time, and, in hindsight, six hours plus some high school Latin may not have been enough.

It went something like this, all in Italian (sort of):

Me: "What think you about the Pope?"

Cousins: "Excuse me? What do you mean? The Pope is the Pope."

Me: "What you think about him? Is he good Pope or bad Pope?" This is the black and white I mentioned.

The cousins started talking to each other, all at the same time, not paying any attention to me. I understood a little when they said "bad Pope" with voices raised in wonder.

Cousins (to me): "The Pope is the Pope"

Me: "Yes, I know. But do you like him?"

The cousins, again amongst themselves, spoke very quickly and all at the same time, a sort of Italian version of *The View.*

Cousins (to me): "Gerardo, the Pope is the Pope. We like him always."

Me: "Like you what he makes?" (I only knew the word for "make," not the one for "do.")

Cousins: "The Pope is the Pope. All is good."

By this time they wore a look on their collective faces that was somewhere between pain and astonishment. I had to get out of this. I wondered how you would say *controversial* or *nontraditional*, but in six hours, those words never came up. I did recall the word for *forced march* from translating Caesar, but somehow that would not fit the situation. Then a way out dawned on me.

> Me: "But he not Italian."
> Cousins: "Oh, Gerardo, no problem, the Pope is the Pope."

With that, the conversation died, and I dared not start another.

A while later the translator returned. The elder women took her aside, and, in an animated fashion at a hundred miles an hour, explained something to her. She nodded her head, came over to me, and said, "They want to know, are you Catholic?"

Olgiate Comasco: Seconda volta

Corned Beef Meets Ravioli

About three months after my first solo trip to Italy to meet my cousins, the entire family, traveled down to see them as a unit. The Queen, the two princesses, and I made the three-hour car trip through the Alps from our town in northern Switzerland.

I may not have mentioned the reception I received the first time. I was like the prodigal son. One of my grandfather's sisters was still alive. Because he moved to the United States before she was born, and I was named Gerard after him, she saw me as her brother incarnate. In a way, I had a similar feeling, since my grandfather died six months before I was born. I was, in a sense, meeting him for the first time through the family. One Gerard visits another long-gone Gerardo.

The woman I married, who is often referred to in these pages as the Queen, is not of Italian descent but of Irish-German descent. How would the Italian cousins warm up to my blue-eyed wife, and how about my Italian-Irish-German kids? The older princess has an olive complexion and is sort of a female version of the word *Tortorelli*. The younger princess has white skin and has inherited my wife's family's deviated septum.

When they were younger and visitors commented on how different they looked, I would respond, "That's not surprising, since Beth is by my first wife." This statement is totally true, since I've only had one wife. As they grew up, they looked more alike, so I can't use that joke anymore. Pity.

The key to understanding Italians is to know that the Pope is number one, family is two, and kids are numbers three, four, five, etc. Within a few minutes of us getting there it became "Gerardo who?" Susan, Beth, and Lynne were the stars. At one point someone even said, "Susan speaks good Italian," which just about made me jump out of my skin, since she was faking the whole thing. Italians are so expressive that you can actually fake knowing the actual language. Sue is good at this.

The highlight of Sue's first visit was The Tour. It is required that all adult family members get the village tour. All the places that are so important in our family history are shown off. I had taken The Tour just a few months prior, but I went along to act as a translator for my wife, who spoke such "good Italian."

One of the homes featured on the tour is no longer inhabited, maybe because it is an extra house in the family that no one needs, or maybe it is that the siblings are still arguing over who gets the house twenty-five years after the last parent has died. It doesn't really matter—this house in my cousin's husband's family was uninhabited. It still qualified for The Tour even though it was an "in-law house." This demonstrates the Italian extended-family concept in action. They showed us the outside and then offered to show us the inside. Susan had accepted the offer without realizing it. When you fake knowing a language, these things happen.

She asked, "Why are we going inside if no one lives here?"

I said, "Because you said you wanted to."

In any case we were on our way inside this house, which was being used as a sewing center for my cousin's little sewing hobby business.

It was a very nice house in its day, but that day was awhile ago. Having been empty of actual inhabitants for close to a generation, there were a number of items that needed attending to. As a place to sew sweaters and assorted other garments it was fine, but you wouldn't want to live there.

Then it happened. You see, if you are expert at faking a language, you can get away with a lot. There, in the foyer of this once stately home, now a dilapidated fabric shop, my wife said it. She did not try to hide it, nor did she try to disguise it. She smiled and looked so pleased, and she said in a loud, bounce-it-off-the-peeling-ceiling voice, "Who lives in this dump?"

The cousins smiled and nodded. They were pleased that she was so pleased. I almost had a heart attack.

To this day, my mother's first cousins have no idea what Susan said. They also have no idea how little she understood of what they said. My only hope is that this little story is translated into Italian some day.

It is amazing how good she is at faking a language. I think that's all she fakes, but you'd have to ask her.

The Italian Telephone Disaster

Since 1982, when I first traveled there to visit, I have been back to see my Italian cousins numerous times. This is one of the advantages of having my office in Switzerland. There are many memorable occasions, some happy, some sad. The 1984 Italian Telephone Disaster, however, stands out among them.

In 1984, we were living in the French-speaking part of Switzerland and preparing to move on to a new assignment in England. It was going to take about two weeks for our furniture to get from the continent to the UK. During that time, we would be housed in company apartments or hotels at company expense. This may sound nice, but with our two princesses, aged seven and five, it was not going to be all that enjoyable.

We came up a better idea for at least part of this in-transition time. We would visit the cousins in Italy. This took on special significance because I was sure that this UK assignment was preparation for a "back home" assignment in North America. This might be the last time we saw the Italian cousins for a while.

Leaving an apartment in Switzerland is not simple. After you officially vacate the flat, there is an inspection, unlike in North America.

In Switzerland, every hole in the wall, every scratch, every piece of lint is noted, and a portion of your deposit is deducted. Hence, when your company moves you, they normally hire a cleaning crew to go over the apartment for a full day of scrubbing and washing, Swiss-style. There is no clean like a Swiss clean.

After our belongings were packed into the trucks and the keys handed over to the cleaning crew, we were off to see the Italian cousins. A colleague had advised me to remove the phone from the apartment. The phone system had not yet been disconnected. The cleaning crew, left in the flat on their own, might call faraway lands, and I wouldn't know until after I was out of the country.

I would never expect this to be a problem in safe, law-abiding Switzerland. My colleague's face turned grim when I questioned his warning, and, in a loud voice, he announced, "Yes. But these cleaning crews are not made up of Swiss. They are all foreigners. Who knows what they would do. Why, they could be from Yugoslavia, Turkey, or Italy." In Switzerland, anything that goes wrong is always the result of "foreigners."

I wanted to remind him what my last name was, but having dealt with this type of Swiss national chauvinism before, I just shook my head. I asked a less biased colleague, and he thought it would not be a bad idea to take the phone. Better safe than sorry. So I unplugged the phone and put it in the trunk. Now down to Italy.

The early 1980s was a time in Europe when some people were thinking of a global language called Esperanto and the "one Europe" concept was just beginning. Then there were the other people. They thought of Europe as it had been for centuries. It's what I call the Darwinist View. "We are all trapped on the same continent; protect everything you've got, and let the fittest survive." The most Darwinist people of all in the 1980s were the border guards, and the worst of the worst were the Italian border guards.

With this in mind, we arrived at the cousins' house and looked forward to four days of relaxation. On the morning of the second day, I made the mistake of asking my cousin where the nearest gas station was. My tank was near empty. "You can't buy gas in Italy," I was told. "It is much cheaper in Switzerland. Let's drive up to the border, get some gas, and come back. It is was only eight kilometers (five miles) up the road."

For some reason, gas and sugar were cheaper in Switzerland than Italy at the time. It had to do with taxes and farm subsidies. There might have been a hundred other such items, but in my cousin's mind, gas and sugar were the key ones. The plan was for him and me to drive across the border about fifty yards, get gas and sugar, and return. They sold sugar at the Swiss gas stations near the Italian border. Even if there were lines at the border, it would take a maximum of twenty minutes. That's why when two hours had gone by and we were not yet back, the rest of the cousins waded deeply into a debate over what might have happened. Italian debates get very loud. Susan was enjoying this without any worry at all. Her contention was that we had stopped for a drink. One Italian cousin thought we might be in jail. He was actually closer to the truth.

The first part of the plan went well. We got into Switzerland, purchased our gas and four kilograms of sugar, and headed back to the border. There an Italian border guard decided he should inspect our car. No problem, I had no contraband. Well, not that I knew of.

After opening the trunk, he found something that made his day—a telephone, specifically a Swiss telephone. Then came a heated argument.

I should tell you at this point that the cousin who accompanied me on our gas and sugar trek was Carlo. Carlo speaks no English; nor did the border guard. This was another pre-Internet European phenomenon.

I was asked to get out of the car, and, to the best of my knowledge; I was asked why I had a phone in the car. I explained that my apartment was being cleaned, and I didn't want people to use the phone. Well, that's what I thought I was saying, but I didn't speak Italian very well, so I wasn't sure what they heard me say. At least I made the attempt. People often say that natives are impressed when you attempt to speak their language. They are not talking about border guards.

I did understand from the hand gestures and limited language knowledge that importing a phone into Italy was not permitted. We would have to leave the phone or return to Switzerland. After fruitlessly arguing with the border guard, my cousin simply nodded to me and we headed back into Switzerland.

Carlo has the reputation of being quite an expressive person who can hold his own in an Italian argument. I was astonished, therefore, when he gave up so quickly and quietly, but he had a plan. You see, in addition to the border crossing at Novazzano where we were, there is a very small one-lane border crossing about a mile down the road. You had to be a local to know where it was. As we found out, you also have to be a local to use it.

This small border crossing looked like something out of a 1940s movie: a shack on the side of the road with a barrier that was moved up and down by hand. Carlo used it all the time and in fact knew the border guard there by name. The border guard said we could not cross into Italy, as I was a foreigner. You had to be Italian or Swiss in order to use that border crossing. He did not have any computer system to check my America passport. Nowadays they have a simple handheld wireless computer. Come to think about it, there are almost no checks on the borders nowadays anyway, so we could have driven through. It was 1984, however. George Orwell was wrong about 1984; Big Brother wasn't watching yet.

I understood the border guard to say that we shouldn't be inconvenienced because all we needed to do was go down about a mile to the border crossing at Novazzano. Little did he know that at Novazzano, we were already known as phone smugglers.

The fact that my cousin was now yelling at the top of his lungs at no one in particular made me think that a heart attack—his—was next on the agenda. Using a map, he showed me where we had to cross: at Chiasso, which was half an hour's drive along the border. This also involved a half an hour return. I understood him to say that Chiasso was the main crossing point; it would be full of traffic from the highway, but we had no choice.

So next we were in Chiasso, waiting in a twenty-minute queue to get to the customs booth. The phone was carefully hidden under my seat. We sat like two choirboys and awaited the questions from the border guard.

I understood the nationality question, which we answered to his satisfaction, and the "Why were you in Switzerland?" question, which

Carlo answered by saying he just wanted to show me the lake. Then came the big one. Are you importing anything? Not mentioning the phone, Carlo matter-of-factly said, "Just four kilograms of sugar."

The border guard said something. Carlo got really aggravated. Both raised their voices, and quickly the speed of the conversation left my Italian skills in the dust. It turns out that we were allowed only one kilogram of sugar per person, two kilograms total. He would have to get rid of the extra two kilograms.

You know, it seemed somewhat fair. I had gone to Switzerland in order to save a few centimes on a liter of gas and ended up using more than that in our trek. Why shouldn't Carlo lose some hard-earned sugar savings as well? However, it was not that simple. You see, we couldn't just leave the sugar at customs. We had to take it back into Switzerland. At this point, the simple half hour round trip was already into its second hour.

So back into Switzerland we went. Wanting to cut our losses, Carlo decided the best thing would be to give the sugar away. You would think that would be easy. But he was in an even more expressively agitated mode than before. I never learned the Italian word for being this angry, but in the Bronx, we might say he was a raving lunatic. Normal people tend to run away from people like this in any language, which made giving the sugar away a chore. We just left it in a trash bin by the side of the road and got back in line.

Fifteen minutes later we were in front of the same guard and told him we had disposed of the sugar. He let us through without an inspection. That incensed Carlo more; he felt betrayed. If he knew that the guy was going to take our word for it, he would have hid it under my seat next to the phone and not left the sugar in Switzerland.

When we returned to the homestead, the discussion was in full swing. Now the Carlo could give them the inside scoop, blow by blow. The decibel level was about as high as a 747 taking off. Everyone seemed to have an answer to our dilemma after the fact, and, of course, all agreed that we had done it wrong, which really helped Carlo get even more excited.

We left Italy by the Novazzano border crossing two days later. The first stop we made when we entered Switzerland was at a gas station. I had used up all my cheap gas on our trek.

Rome: I'll have nun of it

It was clear. Before we moved back to North America from Switzerland, we were going to see Rome. We knew it, and of course our Italian cousins knew it. The issue was that we couldn't just go to Rome and stay in a hotel when we had a distant cousin living in Rome. We were obliged to stay with this cousin, whom we didn't even know.

I really didn't want to impose on some third or fourth cousin, but there was no way my Olgiate cousins were going to let us go to Rome without staying at Cousin Francesca's.

The entire conversation about our Rome trip went on in Italian. We were assured many times that Cousin Francesca had "lots of room." It would not be an inconvenience, we were told. That was easy for the Olgiate cousins to say, being three hundred miles north of Rome. Poor Cousin Francesca might have a different view. I assumed that she would sleep on the floor while she let us sleep in her bed. Every time we had visited the Olgiate cousins, they went out of their way to make us feel at home, even giving up their beds for us. This only made me feel more ill at ease.

The Olgiate cousins made us promise that before we booked the Rome trip, we would call them, and they would make sure there was a place to stay with Cousin Francesca. For a brief moment, the Queen and I entertained going off on our own. "Don't call them," I insisted. "Let's do it and plead we never went to Rome." For the sake of family harmony, we finally decided to make the call to the Olgiate cousins and bite the bullet. If we wanted to see Rome, we were going to stay with Cousin Francesca.

To make sure everything was clearly understood, we asked a neighbor who spoke Italian to help with the call, which took place around mid-day. Imagine my surprise when I got home from work. The Queen had called the cousins and was ready with the scoop on our trip to Rome. I couldn't wait.

"Are we going to Rome?" I asked.

"Yes," the Queen answered.

"Are we staying with Cousin Francesca?"

"Yes," the Queen said again.

My heart sank. I was resigned that my trip to Rome would not be the freewheeling, discover-Rome trip I had dreamed of but instead be complicated by feeling we were imposing on some poor distant relative.

"Don't worry, Cousin Francesca has lots of space," the Queen said, with a smile that indicated she knew something I didn't. I think they teach that in royalty school.

Then she continued. "It seems your cousin Francesca is actually your grandmother's cousin."

Well, that was better. Maybe she was an empty nester, and we wouldn't be an imposition after all.

Then came the real bombshell. "You see, your grandmother's cousin Francesca is a nun, and we are staying at her convent."

This took a second to register. Convent? Nun? Rome?

A month later, off we went. The Queen, the two princesses, and I traveled to Rome and stayed at the Ursuline Convent on the eastern side of the city. It was a memorable trip. Cousin Francesca was a delightful seventy-two-year-old retired nun who was in charge of the kitchen. The convent had a boarding school and, as there were often times when parents would stay over, there were a few apartments for their use. Our small family had a very nice, simply furnished two-bedroom apartment. Every morning you could hear the door open, and if you were quick, you would see the trail of a black and white habit dash in and set up breakfast.

The princesses were seven and five at that time, and they actually stayed at the school one day with the other kids, who spoke only Italian. That day, Sue and I toured parts of Rome that the kids would not have enjoyed: translation—museums.

So our first trip to Rome was indeed a great trip. I like the way the Queen summed it up the best. "Our first trip to Rome, and we got to stay in a convent. Next time, let's hold out for the Pope."

"You no love your wife"

In the days when I was running the U.S. division of our company, I would go the head office in Switzerland about four times per year. Often my Chief Financial Officer would join me, as the Swiss always seemed to want to know something about money. On one specific occasion, my VP of manufacturing also joined us, as we were asking for a wad of cash with which to upgrade our factory. It seemed we had to have a plan before they signed off on the capital. Go figure.

We arrived on a Wednesday to face two days of intense meetings, in which we reviewed every drawing and plan for what we were going to do to bring this factory into the twenty-first century. By the time Friday afternoon rolled around, we had enough of the Swiss and wanted to get away from it all for a while before having to repeat the fight again on Monday.

The CFO had the idea to spend the weekend in Italy. It would be relaxing and, he added, the hotel rooms would be cheaper. So off we went, a set of three musketeers: Dan, Tom, and I. Dan and I are of Italian origin, so in order to make sure Tom didn't feel left out, we started adding an *o* to his last name. I don't think he was impressed. Besides, his blond hair cried out his real name, Shoup rather than the Shoupo we had christened him. Shoupo also sounded a little like a Marx brother.

Tom may not be Italian, but he is a romantic. He comes from California, so maybe that has something to do with it. In any case, he called his wife and asked what she would like him to bring her from northern Italy. He did so before telling us. We would have counseled against it. All the wives know each other, and asking one wife a question like that leads to the others wanting to know why their husband didn't ask.

Tom's wife answered that she would like some leather goods, as that is what the area is known for. She thought that maybe a pocketbook would be nice. The die was cast. We were to spend our weekend shopping for a purse.

We had a pleasant trip through the Alps. We had decided to stay in the northern Italian town of Stresa, on Lago Maggiore, mostly because we had heard that the restaurants were good and it was close. I had been there before, so I knew the lay of the land. Arriving in the town on Friday evening, we looked at a few hotels and found an elegant one. The CFO had been right that the hotel rates were better in Italy. That's why he was the CFO. A good meal, some wine and grappa: the weekend was starting well.

On Saturday morning, Tom wanted to get his shopping done, so we headed into the back streets, which were laden with shops.

Soon we came upon a particular leather goods shop featuring mainly pocketbooks, with a smattering of wallets and belts thrown in. Tom seemed to know what he wanted. I started inside with him while he looked over the merchandise. Then I meandered outside to look at the wares on the pocketbook trees outside the store. While the husband of this husband-and-wife team of shop owners was serving Tom, the wife was outside watching me.

Dan, the CFO, was enjoying a cigarette from a good distance away. This gave him a very clear view of what was going on. He saw Tom inside and me outside, each with one of the owners nearby. I really wasn't interested in shopping for a pocketbook for the Queen, but if something caught my eye, I might be tempted.

The key sales pitch that the owners used was based on the fact that the better pocketbooks used larger pieces of better leather. The best ones used only one piece for the entire body of the purse. There would be the minimum of seams in such a pocketbook, and all the leather was first quality. They would also be one consistent color. Tom liked that idea and proceeded to look at some of these rather expensive items. I, on the other hand, was looking at the cheaper pocketbooks, which were made from numerous pieces of brown leather, all tanned slightly different shades. I actually liked the look. It would fit the Queen on the days when she decided not to be so regal.

From afar, Dan could see what was happening. As soon as Tom started to look at the $140 purses, the wife-owner came over to me and started to talk me up in price, using the fact that my friend was willing to get his wife something really good and expensive.

I just wanted something different, like a multicolored pocket book. She, however, insisted that it would be an insult to buy my wife such a cheap item. I was informed that the purses I was looking at were made with the scraps left over from the good pocketbooks. Had she known Tom worked for me, she probably would have said, "How could you let you wife be seen with a pocketbook inferior to that of Tom's wife?"

She used the wrong tactic. I would have fallen for the pitch that these multi-piece purses were more expensive because more labor went into them. She didn't use that one—too bad for her.

Finally, having no success, she took the purse I was holding, looked directly at me, and said in rather loud broken English, "You give this to wife, then you no love your wife. Not good. Buy better one." Then she threw the purse onto the ground. She certainly knew how to have an impact.

I guess it sort of worked, because I did buy a slightly better pocketbook. It was still a multi-piece, multicolored one. Okay, she talked me up to a $50 purse from a $35 one. Dan, who observed it all, says she intimidated me into getting the better one. I say, who wants to buy a purse that has been thrown on the ground?

Bang your head on a coffin

One day early in March 2004, during the time I was living in the United States but working in Switzerland, I visited my cousins in Italy. I had driven down for the weekend from my hotel outside of Zürich. One of the cousins asked when I would be back, and I said, "Sometime in April." He suggested that I come on April 25th so I could "bang my head on the coffin." Since this conversation was going on in English, I knew I had heard him correctly, but I still didn't understand his meaning.

He explained a bit. It seems there is a custom in our town in Italy about going to Monza in adoration of Saint Gerardo. He said I would have to experience it. What the heck. I decided to come back in late April and take part in something to do with a saint, a coffin, and a "male cow." This is the story.

Every year on April 25, the entire town of Olgiate-Comasco in northern Italy is invited to the Church of Saint Gerardo in Monza. By tradition, every family should be represented. This church houses the remains of Saint Gerardo del Tintori. Although there is a small Saint Gerardo church in Olgiate itself, the saint's body is in the larger one in Monza. Like everything in Italy, there is a fantastic story behind it all.

In 1207, it seems a plague of sorts affected Olgiate. A wise old man was consulted and said that they should ask for Gerardo's help. Since he was already dead, that actually meant praying to him. In his lifetime, Gerardo had been a nobleman of some wealth who turned to helping the poor. He founded hospitals for the poor in the area—sort of a Mother Theresa of the thirteenth century.

The entire town prayed to him, and the disease went away. This sickness was described as a serious "malady of the head." From what can be gleaned from the history books, it was something like a meningitis epidemic. You can imagine the jokes about mental illness and Olgiate, however.

In appreciation for what Gerardo had done for Olgiate, the town pledged that a representative of each family would travel each year to his burial place in Monza. Monza is the town where the Formula 1 racetrack is.

After Gerardo became Saint Gerardo del Tintori, this pilgrimage became even more important. One of the miracles used to prove his sainthood was in fact the curing of Olgiate-Comasco. Others included using his cape to help people cross a flooded river.

You would think that his body would be somewhere in Olgiate. So did most of the Olgiatesi (inhabitants of Olgiate). There was a constant argument between the two towns, Monza and Olgiate, on who should get his remains. Somewhere along the way, they decided to settle this once and for all in a truly Italian fashion.

They dug up poor Saint Gerardo and put his body in a wagon pulled by a male cow (really a bull, but my translator called it a "male cow," so in deference to him I'll call it that too). If the cow went toward Olgiate, they got the body. If it went toward Monza, they got it. The Olgiatesi still believe it was fixed—sort of like hanging chads, 1592-style.

To make up for not having the body, Olgiate built the Church of St. Gerardo (much smaller than the one in Monza). This is where the weddings, funerals, and baptisms for our family have been going on since the early 1600s. One of the highlights of the church's history took place in 1946, when the body of Saint Gerardo traveled to Olgiate for the first time. It was there only a short period and was then returned to the tomb in Monza.

In modern times, entire families often make the trip together. Some people make the pilgrimage on foot, while others bike down in groups. Most people drive the forty-two kilometers (twenty-six miles) in private cars. This particular year, five buses were rented for the trip as well. In the mid-1960s, when many families did not have their own cars, a record was set when thirty buses were used for the trip. I estimated from the inside of the church that more than 3,500 people attended the mass. Remember the town has about 11,000 inhabitants.

Tradition dictates that the first time you make the trip, you should put three leaves on the Lion Bridge in Monza. Since I didn't do this, I may be going directly to hell, but I tried to fulfill the rest of the customs required.

Public access to the coffin is allowed only twice per year: on June 6, his feast day, and on the Olgiate pilgrimage day, April 25. The public is invited to view the coffin after the pilgrims' mass in the main church. The coffin sits in a room above one of the side altars in the church.

Saint Gerardo's coffin is glass, allowing you to see his bones. Saint Gerardo is dressed in finery, and a crown is on his head. The only portions of his skeleton one can see are his hands, forearms, and head. All the bones are fleshless dark brown. His teeth are still white, which is eerie in itself. The tradition calls for you to tap your head on the glass coffin and ask for cures to any head disease you may encounter.

The staircase up to his tomb is narrow and winding, as is its mirror copy going down. You exit into the courtyard of the church into a throng of Olgiatesi, most of whom are related to me in some fashion or other. There you buy a small bottle of wine and loaf of bread. This is in honor of the people of Monza, who began giving the pilgrims from Olgiate bread and wine sometime in the sixteenth century.

You may ask why the pilgrimage takes place on April 25th. In fact, it has only been on April 25th since the end of the World War II. You see, the Italians are very practical. They want as many families to take part as possible. It makes sense to choose a day when everyone would be off from work. April 25 is the national holiday of Liberation Day; the day the government of Benito Mussolini was overthrown.

I made my first Saint Gerardo pilgrimage in 2004 and returned in 2005 with the Queen. It has been one of the most memorable things I have ever taken part in. I was not able to make it for the 700th anniversary in 2007.

To think it has been going on for centuries and that my grandfather, who died six months before I was born, made the pilgrimage himself. The last time he would have made it was when he was twelve, just before he came to America. By the way, he was named Gerardo in honor of this wealthy nobleman who cared for the poor and died in 1207. I carry his name as well.

A book has been written about Olgiate's relationship with Saint Gerardo. My cousin Italo gave me a copy prior to his death. The book is entitled *San Gerardo e Olgiate, un Santo e un popolo* (*Saint Gerardo and Olgiate, a saint and a people*). I treasure this, even though I can't read it that well. You see, it came from a cousin.

Postscript: Growing up, I had a statue of Saint Gerard on my dresser. I still have it to this day. It rests in a drawer now, though. It is a statue of a priest who I was told was the patron saint of pregnant women. The devotion to this Saint Gerard is quite strong. I even know a woman whose middle name is Gerard because her mother prayed to Saint Gerard to help her become pregnant.

When I made the pilgrimage in 2004, I noticed that Saint Gerardo was a nobleman. Was my statue incorrect? Yes and no. The more famous Saint Gerardo, the one who is indeed the patron of mothers-to-be, is Saint Gerardo Majella, from southern Italy. Ours is Saint Gerardo del Tintori. Hey, we beat the other guy by five hundred years, so I call ours Saint Gerardo, the First.

The savior, a rice dish, and a traffic jam resolved

I always enjoy attending religious services in other languages. When I am in Switzerland, I go to mass at St. Peter and Paul Church in Winterthur, just north of Zürich. I still contest that since the church is named after two saints, every mass I attend should count as two Sundays' worth. My friend Father Michael doesn't agree. I argued with him once, but I gave up when he mentioned something about excommunication.

In 2007, I was happy to go to Easter Mass in my family's hometown in northern Italy. The church is the same one that my grandfather was baptized in and the one he attended until the age of thirteen when he came to the United States: St. Gerardo. My grandfather's name was Gerardo, and mine is the English equivalent. Looking around at the walls, I am always struck by the sense that he was once in this place. I can imagine him as a child sitting in the pew.

I also live in the present. This specific present was an Easter Mass celebrated in Italian. I had my English missal, so I could follow along with the readings and prayers. It always puts a smile on my face when I am able to translate as I read the English and hear the Italian. One reason I feel so accomplished in doing this is that growing up, I only learned Italian curse words or words dealing with food. Any bible reading is sure to offer a new vocabulary beside what I learned as a child. Until this Easter Mass, that is.

Easter is a solemn feast. It is what Christianity is based on. I was merrily following along until the gospel. Then it happened, right in the middle of the reading according to St. Luke. The priest said "risotto."

I happen to make a mean risotto and often compare recipes with others in Italy. It is my signature dish. So the mention of risotto in the Easter gospel was, I though, either some joke by the priest or a mistake. Since no one was laughing, I decided that it was an oversight by the priest. Why else would I hear risotto in the middle of the gospel?

A minute or so later, I heard it again. Then I heard it at least six times in the homily. Still no laughter. This was odd. Maybe the church had rented out the facility for a rather solemn cooking class. Was Emeril hiding around the corner of the baptistery?

This was perplexing to say the least. Like most things that occur in my head, I built it up to a real dilemma. I couldn't figure out how a rice dish made with saffron and chicken stock found its way into the service. It would have been more appropriate if they had designated which type of risotto it was: "risotto Milanese" or "risotto con fungi," but all that was said was "risotto." I was wondering what type of risotto would have made it into the Jewish Passover celebration that was celebrated at the Last Supper.

Then came the big one. Near the end of the homily, the priest said, in a very loud voice, meant to have an impact, "Christo e risotto!" Translation: "Christ is an Italian rice dish." Everyone seemed to be pleased, and some people even yelled a very distinctive "Amen," which lead me believe that they let some Italian Baptists in for good measure.

"Christo e risotto!" My mind was working overtime, but still I couldn't figure it out. I wondered if the Spanish say, "Christ is paella."

Was the devil causing me to hear a food term when I shouldn't? Was it a sign from the most high that I should dedicate my life to making risotto for the poor and under-riced people of the world? I was perplexed.

Besides the Queen, there were at least eight female cousins in attendance at this mass, so I had a list of family members to check with. It seems that most Italian men in our family do not go to mass, but that's okay; the women would be better witnesses. They would have been paying attention.

Back at the cousins' house, I had my chance. First, I asked the Queen, "Did you hear the word *risotto* in the sermon and gospel today?" She gave me a strange look and decided it was not an answerable question.

I dove in and asked my cousins. "Why did the priest say *risotto* at mass?" Here again I got the look that is reserved for situations like this. It is the "what-language-are-you-speaking" look. I explained that I distinctively heard risotto mentioned at least eight times. The older women started to move away from me, and I think they were considering re-asking the "are-you-Catholic" question from years before. Then one of my cousins figured it out. It was *risorto,* not *risotto.* Then everyone laughed and started treating me as if I was sane again.

The reason risorto was not seen to be inappropriate at mass was that it means risen. "Christo e risorto" is "Christ is risen," not "Christ is an Italian rice dish." That explains why the priest did not add "con fungi" or "Milanese" at the end.

I was once diagnosed with what is called a lazy tongue. That means that I do not pronounce my *r*'s well. When I was younger, I even went to speech classes for a while. My *r*'s are good enough now for English, but in Italian they do not have enough roll to them. In German, the issue is even worse. I guess I must have lazy ears as well, since I don't seem to hear some *r* sounds. Therefore, as they were telling me he said risorto, not risotto, I had a hard time seeing the difference. Italians can evidently tell the difference.

This was all well and good, and the cousins had another crazy-Gerardo story to tell their friends, but it got worse. After Easter, the Queen, my sister, her daughter, and I toured Florence and Venice for a few days' vacation. I was the driver during this sojourn. On the highway between Florence and Bologna are electronic signs that let you know the condition of traffic ahead.

The first sign indicated that there had been a problem at kilometer marker 227, but it added "INCIDENTE RISOTTO." Wait a second. Had an Uncle Ben's truck turned over, spilling its rice contents over the autostrada? Upon further inspection, I saw that it actually said "INCIDENTE RISOLTO," meaning "accident resolved."

Sometimes in North America, I now ask for risotto but actually say "risorto." It's my little joke. Waiters don't hear the difference. I am the only one who knows I just ordered a side dish of "risen." The question is, is it risen "con fungi" or "Milanese"?

Baby on board

I don't know who came up with the first BABY ON BOARD sign that you see in car windows. It was popular a number of years ago in North America. Offshoots of it have developed over the years. Things like "True believer on board" or "Adult on board." There might even be one that announces "Topless dancer on board" for all I know. It seems that everyone wanted to be "on board" for a while.

Enter my niece Kristin, my sister Laura's daughter, who is soon having my mother's first great-grandchild. Kristin does everything to the *n*th degree. She always has and always will. She lives life to the fullest. I am sure she will have a BABY ON BOARD sign. In fact, I sort of expect that her car will look a little like it belongs in a NASCAR race. She may have "baby on board" painted on the roof.

All new parents are proud, no matter what country they live in, so I assume the BABY ON BOARD sign exists in many countries. I haven't seen it in Switzerland, but the Swiss are a little conservative anyway. I have seen it in Italy, however. Well, you understand that it is in Italian, but it is the same sentiment: "baby on board."

We are a close-knit family, and as such, we are always looking for things to buy for other members of the family. When my oldest sister and her daughter Ann joined the Queen and me on a trip to Italy this year, we, of course, were on the lookout for things that we could buy for Kristin's soon-to-be-born baby. A bib from Florence was one item we thought a newborn had to have. We never thought of a BABY ON BOARD sign, until we saw one in Como.

As soon as she saw it, Ann had to have one for her cousin. Ann is a generous, giving person, but that is not why she wanted to have an Italian BABY ON BOARD sign for her cousin. She was into it for the fun of it—the fun she would get from seeing this on her cousin's car.

Even my sister got into the act, asking in a toy store if they had such a sign. Of course, she asked in Venice and the lady responded. "But Signora, we do not have cars here."

You would think that the Italian sign would read something like BAMBINO A BORDO, but it doesn't. For some reason they use the pet name for bambino, *bimbo*. The sign that Ann saw, the one my sister wanted for Kristin reads BIMBO A BORDO. Not exactly "topless dancer on board," but close. Let's see if Kristin paints that on the roof.

Postscript: When I originally wrote this in 2006, I envisioned it as part of a longer piece dedicated to the five cousins who are my mother's five granddaughters, Ann, Kristin, Carol, Beth and Lynne. They were as close as cousins can be, even though they have lived far apart over the years.

On November 21, 2008, my niece Kristin, the one I write about in this story, was killed in an automobile accident near her home in Maryland. She was thirty-four, and she left behind her husband Chris and her daughter Isabelle, who was two and a half when Kristin passed away.

I told Kristin about this story once, and she laughed. If you knew her, that's what you would expect her to do.

5. Our home and not-so-native land

Welcome to Canada... eh?

O Canada

In July of 1985, we emmigrated from the UK to Canada. The princesses were seven and six years old. We were not exactly coming home, but at least we were on the same continent as our family. The family was still eight hours away, but this time a visit meant a drive instead of a flight.

As it turned out, we spent twelve years in "the true north, strong and free."* In the end, we became citizens, so indeed for us "we stand on guard for thee."* Both of my daughters and their families reside there now. It is Canada now that feels more like home in many ways.

Our story in Canada is the story of our children, because they did most of their growing up there. The Queen and I moved back to the States when our youngest went off to college. Canada was and still is a great place to raise children. At some point, we may end up back in "our home and native land."*

In Canada, I was president of the local Ringette Association, a form of girls' ice hockey, yet I do not skate. I was the head of the first parish council in the new church we joined, yet I do not consider myself that great a Catholic. I was president of my first company, yet I am still a kid from the Bronx. Finally, I became a curler, a game I never knew existed until moving to Canada.

If you would have told me when I was a kid that I would one day become a citizen of another country, I probably would have punched you out. Our Canadian experience, however, changed all that. You see, "true patriot love in all thy sons command."*

When George Bush the First was running for president, he made a statement that he wanted to have a "kinder, gentler America." The joke was it already exists—Canada. Don't get me wrong; there are a lot of things that need fixing, and some aggravate me, about our adopted land, but Canada has a lot going for it. It reminds me of what I believed the United States was all about when I was young.

Our stay in Canada was so important to our family that I should devote an entire book to it. Maybe I will.

(Note: the quotes marked with an * are taken from the Canadian National Anthem, *O Canada*)

A pregnant nun and a chicken at mass

Upon our arrival in Canada, we enrolled the girls in the local Catholic grammar school. In Ontario, the Catholic Schools are run by the Separate School Board and paid for out of taxes. The secular schools are run by the regular school board and are also paid for by the government. Any other denomination, Jewish, Protestant, Muslim etc, are not supported by the government. It all goes back to the history of Canada, which is a history of English versus French, which was a history of Protestant versus Catholic. Catholic education is in the Constitution, while no other religion's education is. It's a typically Canadian thing.

We registered the family in the Catholic parish in the neighboring town and were informed that soon "they" would be starting a new parish in our town. I remember thinking; I wonder who "they" are. It turned out I was one of the "they."

The new parish, St. Justin, Martyr, was holding mass in the gym at one of the schools. After one Sunday when I didn't attend mass, the Queen came home and informed me that she nominated me to run the first ever St. Justin, Martyr, parish picnic. I made a mental note that I would never miss mass again.

Running the picnic was fun. It evolved into me being on the first-ever parish council and, in fact, being the first-ever president of the parish council. Boy, this was some penance for missing mass that day.

In starting a new faith-based community, there are two goals: build the community and then build the facility. The first is the most important, but the second is a way to accomplish the first. Working together to build the church structure helped us all become a community.

We needed a little over two and a half million dollars for the church/rectory complex that we wanted to build. Having a priest who sat on the archdiocese building committee as our pastor gave us an insight into what we had to do. Committees were set up, and we interviewed a number of professional fundraisers to determine whom to use. The shock was that these organizations took about a third of what they raised as their fee. We would end up doing most of the work to boot.

Remember this was in a suburb of Toronto, where many of the parishioners were execs for major companies. We had a variety of skills to draw from. We had accountants, marketing guys, sales people, and even the head of the flavor company (that would be me). I figured if they ever wanted to flavor the communion hosts, my skills could come in handy. We decided in the end to do it ourselves—not the flavored communion thing but the fundraising thing.

We gleaned from the professional fundraisers that it was important to get as many people involved in the organization and implementation of the fundraising as possible. Once people were involved, they would feel a sense of ownership in both the parish and the fundraising activity. This would lead them to write bigger donation checks. It's nice to have bake sales and sell poinsettias at Christmas, but in reality, such activities raise a very small percentage of what's needed. It's the donations that pay the way, and any activity should include a sense of community to enhance the sense of ownership.

The fundraising project was given a name: Project Pioneer. We had a logo developed and slogan; *A new beginning … an adventure for all.* Pins were printed, brochures developed, pledge sheets produced, and labels made that we stuck on everything. We were very conscious of our brand.

The professional fundraisers stressed that we should use a big event as a kick-off. This event would not be a fundraiser at all. In fact it would cost us money, not make us money. The purpose was to get everyone involved, either to attend the event or help to put it on.

As our big event, we choose a theatrical performance, partly because we couldn't think of anything else to do. I volunteered to write and direct it, partly because I was not thinking at the time. So you see not thinking was a big part of the plan.

The name we chose for the big event was The Main Event, which in fact it was. We wanted it to take place right before the canvassing for pledges began. This put it at the end of November 1987: November 30, to be exact.

I wrote an eleven-act musical variety show that included ten funny skits or musical numbers and one very serious multi-projector slide show presentation with a prerecorded professional announcer's voice. It was during the slide show that we made our pitch for donations.

The slides were all about the community that we had been establishing during the two years that the parish had been housed in the gym.

Before the show, we had a cocktail hour with free wine, beer, soda, and some snacks. Luckily, I didn't have to worry about that part. Let me tell you, it takes a lot to produce a show; even a nonprofessional, parish-based one.

The skits were a true mix of ridiculous songs and situational comedy. In each case there was a message; we need a church. There were the "Twelve O'clock Mass Blues," which used the tune from Crystal Gail's "Don't It Make My Brown Eyes Blue" to talk about how hard it was to stack the chairs after the noon mass in the gym.

There was the *Parish Feud* game show, our version of *Family Feud*; in ours, we had the Christians versus the Pagans. One of the answers to the question, "What reminds you of church?" was "Basketball hoop, because this question was asked at St. Justin's where they have their services in a gym."

We had a real mix of talent as well. One of our parishioners was an ex-opera singer, and she did the "Twelve O'clock Mass Blues" and a tribute to a fictitious couple who would be married in the church, called "Wait 'til the Church is Built, Nellie." (To the tune of "Wait 'til the Sun Shines, Nellie.")

The other major talent was a guy who played at the young people's mass every week. He started us all off with "King of the Pioneers," a tribute to our pastor to the tune of "The Ballad of Davey Crocket." It was a good link between the Project Pioneer theme and our show. Fess Parker never dreamed of lyrics like; "Born in Toronto before the war, played himself some hockey with saves galore, the defense he played wasn't very loose, and that's how he got the nickname of Moose."

We had the *Juskateers* (a parody of the *Mouskateers*), *The Gym Shop Quartet* (they did a few songs on raising money for the church), and a *Nun on the Street Interview* (a slide show with a pregnant nun driving a Porsche). We even included a few fictitious commercials, *The First National Bank of HIM* and *One Sacred Chicken to Go*, which were loosely based on a Don Imus album.

I was the writer and director. I did, however, get "on stage" prior to The Main Event. We decided that we needed to promote the event.

We went on local TV and made the point that this was not a fundraiser but a fun raiser.

I also spoke at each mass the three weeks prior to The Main Event. I informed the parish that over the next three weeks they would see three spirits of The Main Event—sort of a *Christmas Carol* prelude.

The first Sunday saw me as a pioneer in a rented Davey Crocket outfit. On the second Sunday, I was a basketball player who shot a ball at the hoop in the main aisle of our gym/church. The last Sunday, I was the *One Sacred Chicken to Go*, in a chicken outfit.

Over one thousand people attended, with 138 volunteers involved in the show in some way or other. The result was fantastic; we set a then-record for the Archdiocese of Toronto in raising funds. We spent in excess of nine thousand dollars to put on the whole shebang. But the community building aspect was exceptional.

I figure if I get to the pearly gates and entrance into heaven is determined by a talent contest, I will belt out my *Gym Shop Quartet* version of "Dough-a-church" to the tune of "Doe-a-deer" from *The Sound of Music*. It goes like this:

> *Dough— is what we need to build*
> *Our— new church in Unionville*
> *If—we all pitch in and give*
> *It— will help to pay the bill*
> *When— your neighbor comes to call*
> *Please— be generous and pledge*
> *Then— we'll have all that we need*
> *Which is dough, dough, dough, dough, dough.*

I told you the message was not subtle.

My pinky ring, a Canadian thing

I don't like pinky rings. I always considered them to be the most garish display of jewelry ever invented. I could not foresee any reason in the world why I would wear a pinky ring, ever. However, as I write this, in the year of our Lord 2006, in a café in Winterthur, Switzerland, I admit I am wearing a pinky ring.

It's rather simple. It has no diamonds or gems of any kind. It is not made of gold or silver or any precious metal. In fact, it has no obvious monetary value at all. It is simple stainless steel, meant to be worn by a select few on the pinky of the working hand: the right hand, in my case. It is not any iron ring. It is the Iron Ring.

It all began in Canada in 1922. At a meeting of past presidents of the Engineering Institute of Canada, a ceremony was established for new engineers as a commitment to ethics: a sort of engineers' Hippocratic Oath. The group asked Rudyard Kipling to develop a ceremony. He came up with what he called, "The Ritual of the Calling of an Engineer." It still carries that name today, and the ceremony remains much the same.

The Iron Ring is worn on the little finger of the working had. The engineer who wears it must have been "obligated at an authorized ceremony of the Ritual of the Calling of an Engineer." Graduates of an engineering program are invited to be obligated near the time of their graduation. There are twenty-five camps administering The Ritual throughout Canada. It is mostly a Canadian thing, but there are some camps in the United States that administer the Ritual as well.

I received my engineering degree in 1972. At that time, I had never been to Canada and had no idea that the Iron Ring existed. Fast-forward twenty-eight years to the spring of 2000. My eldest princess, Beth, was graduating from a Canadian university with an engineering chemistry degree. I graduated as a chemical engineer, so the apple indeed did not fall far from the tree. She told us about the Iron Ring and was very proud that she would be getting hers soon. It is certainly a badge of honor.

We expected to attend the Ritual to see her get her ring. I had heard that an existing engineer would have the honor of putting the ring on the finger of the new engineer. I hoped that maybe I could place my daughter's ring on her. Then we were informed that it didn't work that way. It was a closed ceremony, with only the new engineers and engineers who already had rings taking part. In fact, an obligated engineer, one with a ring already, must put the ring on the new engineer's finger.

I thought it would be a great surprise for her if I got obligated prior to Beth's ceremony and then secretly attended hers to put the ring on her finger. After making several calls and sending copies of my diplomas to the Warden in charge of the ring ceremony, I was told I could get a ring as an "experienced engineer." The only time possible was at the exact same ceremony in Kingston, Ontario, at which my daughter would be obligated.

I accepted and took part along with four other experienced engineers. Beth did not notice me in the crowd because the experienced guys came in last. One of the organizers said he would come to our group and "ring" me first so I could go off to find my daughter.

The place was a gymnasium-like building that was jam-packed with five hundred or so new engineers. All stood on the floor of the gymnasium. After the speeches and the touching ceremony, my new friend, the organizer, came to me and slipped the ring on my finger. It took me a few minutes to find the group Beth was in; when she saw me, she was a bit confused. She probably would not put it past me to crash the ceremony. Then I held up my pinky and explained I was now an obligated engineer.

The Canadians and their British cousins are very good at this type of ceremonial thing. Their traditions are very meaningful and always touching. Had Tolkien not used the name already, it could have been called "The Fellowship of the Ring." It is truly a fellowship.

When I notice the ring on my hand, I don't think of the four years of university that resulted in my engineering degree. Nor do I think of the engineering jobs I have had since. I think of my daughter, and that, you see, is what makes this simple, inexpensive stainless steel ring so priceless.

Wedding toe

I told the story earlier in this book about the only time I was a best man at a wedding. At the time I gave that toast, I believed that it would be the only speech I would ever make at a wedding. I should not have worried, because we have two daughters, the princesses, and we lived in Canada.

Canadians have adopted the customs of their British relatives in making wedding speeches. At most Canadian weddings there are between three and seven speeches. The good weddings keep these short and lighthearted. The bad ones get long, syrupy, and sentimental. Usually most of the speeches are elongated toasts, lasting two to four minutes. The three "keynote speakers" are the parents of the groom, the parents of the bride, and the couple themselves. I say "parents," but often only one parent speaks. I was chosen as the speaker at both of my daughters' nuptials.

The Queen had two strict rules for me regarding both speeches. I think the first one was something about keeping it to ten minutes or less. I am not sure; she only told me that rule once, and I quickly forgot it. I am sure about rule number two, which was clearly communicated to me and anyone else who would listen numerous times per day in the weeks leading up to the weddings. It was simple: no drinking before my speech. Don't get me wrong; the guests, all 15,000 or so of them, seemed to be able to drink from the moment they arrived at the reception. It was just me, the father of the bride and the one, I might add, paying the bill, who could not drink until my oratory responsibilities were fulfilled. Needless to say, I was in favor of giving my speech as early in the dinner as possible.

In defense of this seemingly unrealistic position by the Queen, I must admit that we had been present for a situation where this unfollowed rule resulted in the father of the bride going on for what seemed to be hours about details that were at best embarrassing. At worst, they might have caused the groom to run for the hills. That incident made a lasting impression on the Queen, and so the no-drinking-before-the-speech rule was born.

If this were a democracy, the Queen would also refrain from drink alongside me in a show of support. I knew that was not going to happen within minutes of arriving, when I saw her with her first Cosmopolitan. Long live the monarchy!

My first wedding speech experience came in 2001, with the elder of my two princesses, Beth. It went very well, and I think I made a good speech. It had funny parts and serious parts. Only once did I break down. This seems to be required by genuine renaissance fathers of the bride.

I have always hated planned speeches. I didn't realize this until one day when I was lamenting on my lack of preparation to my assistant, Carol. She put me at ease by saying: "Oh, just wing it. That's when you're at your best." She was right. I always dread planned speeches but usually enjoy extemporaneous ones. For my daughters' weddings, however, I was going to prepare speeches. I might improvise a bit, but, in general, I would stick to the plan.

That is, except for the intro, which had to be made up on the spot. As father of the bride and host for the evening, I thought it proper to mention the previous speaker in my introduction. This was especially true because the speaker immediately before me was the father of the groom. Therefore, I wanted to mention something about his speech. This served as a show of respect for him, as well as giving the audience a bridge between the two talks. It is a good practice.

The father of my daughter Lynne's groom made a great speech. He is a natural. In part of it, he detailed how his future daughter-in-law had diagnosed his badly hurt toe a week earlier. Lynne had recently graduated from medical school, so he mentioned that he was impressed that she got the diagnosis right. His "real" doctor had agreed with her. (Note: later we found out they were both wrong.) At the time he told the story, it was fun that this novice doctor had made the right diagnosis.

I decided, on the fly, to use this story to link our two speeches. As part of my intro, I wanted to point out to my daughter's new father-in-law that she was not in training to be a foot doctor.

The intro went something like this: "George, I was impressed with your story about your toe and Lynne's diagnosis. However, you do know she is going to be a gynecologist, don't you?" Laughter erupted.

Then my follow-up: "So, I have one question. Where has your toe been?"

Hey, if I had had a drink I might not have said it. It serves the Queen right, with her silly rules, anyway.

I'll bet $19 on my granddaughter

In November 2007, my eldest princess gave birth to the next generation of royalty. Katelyn was born in a Windsor, Ontario, hospital. This book was 90 percent complete at the time, and thank God it was. It took all the will power I could muster not to start from scratch. I could have called it *The Little Princess* or *Katelyn Reigns*. Maybe the next book.

You can image that we now make the three-hour road trip from Cleveland more often than we used to in the BK (before Katelyn) era. This is good, since it gives me a chance to visit with my miter saw and use the fridge I bought. (You'll read about that later in the book.) In fact, it would be a relaxing time up there if my son-in-law didn't keep on giving me jobs to do. Next trip we are planting his garden.

The trip itself is not a chore, as I love driving. The Queen, however, is not that crazy about driving on her own, especially in winter. This is a bit of a dilemma. If only there was a bus that ran to Windsor from Cleveland.

The state of Ohio has helped us along these lines. Not with a subsidy or a bailout, but by not allowing gambling in the state. Gambling is allowed and promoted in nearby states and in Ontario, but not in Ohio. One of the big casinos is actually in Windsor, where my daughter and Katelyn live. Actually, my son-in-law lives there too, but now, with two royalty in the house, I think his serf status is assured.

The Casino Windsor staff realize they have a large group of gamblers just three hours south of them in Cleveland. They sponsor a bus that runs daily from Cleveland to Casino Windsor. The demand is so high that many days they add an extra bus. The cost is $19 U.S. dollars. When you get off the bus, they give you a chit worth $20 Canadian dollars to gamble with. You sit back and enjoy a movie, or read a paper, or just sleep on your way up to Windsor. They even stop at a rest stop with a Starbucks, the Queen's favorite coffee.

The Queen really doesn't gamble. The bus company doesn't care if you actually go to the casino or not. Most days they are happy to have another body to help fill the bus. The casino evidently doesn't care that much, as they still give her the chit. Most days she is hurrying to see Katelyn, so she doesn't get a chance to gamble.

They do charge her for the return trip if she stays overnight because she is taking a seat on another day, but still, $38 and $20 Canadian back is a deal. The tolls alone are over $14 dollars round trip.

Last election day in Ohio, we voted on a proposition to allow gambling at a proposed casino near Columbus. Actually, I voted for it because I hoped it would bring more jobs to the state. It went down to defeat.

If the proposition had been approved, I knew I would soon become the chauffer to Windsor again. I'm somewhat glad it lost. Not for any personal reason, but you have to think of that poor bus driver on the Windsor run. He could lose his job.

6. Back in the USA: Home Alone

After sixteen years of living outside of the United States, the family Tortorelli came home in 1997. Since the Queen and I were empty nesters by then, we came home alone. Home was not the East Coast any longer but Solon, Ohio, a Cleveland suburb.

We had a new area to discover, new friends to make, and a new life to develop without kids. Of course, there was always room for family and old friends. Oh yes—and more time for each other.

Mr. Schmidt

I have a friend, Stevie. This is not the sort of name that a fifty-something-year-old man normally uses, but Steven and Steve just don't fit him. He is Stevie and has been since I've known him. I have never asked him if he wants to be called Steven or Steve. I'm afraid he'll pick one of them and I'll have to admit we are no longer fifteen years old. Once in a while, he will be Steve when we are in the presence of friends that first met him as an adult. On rare occasions, he will be Steven, but only when I am really mad at him. In all other cases, he is Stevie.

Stevie, a third musketeer, John, and I met in grammar school and became the closest of friends in high school. To give you an idea how close we are, Stevie and I once gave John a shower. The water kind, not the party kind, but that's a previous story, with its own title.

This relationship became even stronger when both Stevie and John married friends of the Queen. All three of us have remained close friends, albeit from afar, throughout the years. We are the type of friends that you can call after a communication lapse and it seems as if you spoke yesterday.

In 1997, I accepted a job in the Cleveland, Ohio, area, which meant moving back to the United States. I happened to mention this Cleveland move to John on the phone one day. I didn't really understand the moment of silence from the other side of the line when I broke the news. Then he followed it with, "Do you know that Steve Schmidt is moving to Cleveland as well?" John had evidently evolved into calling Stevie Steve, but he had to add the last name because John has a son Steven, and I always get confused as to which one he is talking about.

It turned out I would be in the same town as Stevie. We would both be living in a Cleveland suburb, and for the first few months, we were actually neighbors. He had settled in an apartment complex a few hundred yards from the one I was temporarily living in while I searched for an empty nest suitable for the Queen.

It was fun to reunite with an old friend. We found time to meet but made sure that we gave each other the space we needed. We would have dinner at his place or mine or go out to restaurants. Once he even tried my favorite sport, curling, but only once. Stevie was a marathoner, and I think the idea of sliding down the ice with a forty-two-pound piece of granite was not his cup of tea.

After one of our get-togethers, the Queen asked me what we talked about, and, for the life of me, I couldn't say. We would update each other on the kids: he has three and I have two. I would find out superficially whom he might be seeing on the romantic side.

This was never quite enough for the Queen, as she always wanted more info. She accused me of not asking tough questions. What were the details of his last date, for instance? Actually, I don't think men really care that much about their friends' dates. That was his business.

My wife was annoyed at me for not prying into my friend's life. She made a date with him so she could ask all the questions she wanted. Luckily, I was out of town and didn't have to go through the Queen's version of the Spanish Inquisition.

There was a short time when the Queen assumed that her duty was to set him up with a woman. In her earlier days, she always assumed herself to be the ultimate matchmaker. One of the dates that she arranged for Steve in Cleveland was at our house for a Super Bowl party. I use the name "Steve" here, as the Queen had informed me that "Stevie" sounded too "high-schoolish" in front of his date. I can't remember if it lead to additional dates. I have blocked all this out of my memory. Ask the Queen; she probably has all the details written down.

Stevie did leave us with many Cleveland memories, including what became a very large plant. He is an avid botanist with a permanently green thumb. As a house-warming gift, he gave us a jade plant. That was twelve years ago, and every Christmas, when we move it to place a small pinecone tree in its spot, I get a hernia. I have taken to calling the plant Stephan (*ph* pronounced as an *f*) in honor of Stevie. Something that big has to have a name. The only issue might be that Stephan was my fallback name if Stevie ever insisted that I stop calling him Stevie. Now with the plant named Stephan, that would be problematic.

About this time, I made my first trip to Las Vegas. I was dragged along against my will because the Queen decided that it was a good time to go on vacation with her family. One of the highlights for me was going to magic school. I was out to make my mark in the magic world. Once back in Ohio, I tried my tricks out on friends and some co-workers.

The tricks never had the wow factor I expected, except with Stevie. He had come over one weekend. It must have been during the time that our humidifier was not working, since we were both very thirsty. He drank gin. I drank vodka. After a few drinks, I showed him my magic trick. That is when I discovered what had been missing in my magic career up until then: a drunk audience. Now I only perform when there is an open bar.

As it turned out, Stevie moved back to New Jersey and met a wonderful woman. They complete each other. Stevie has the perpetual green thumb, and Rona once watered a plant for a few months before she realized it was plastic.

They have a gigantic fish tank that has about five fish in it. They collect coral. An exciting evening is sitting in front of the tank with a flashlight to watch the coral open and close. And he didn't like curling.

Now they have a dog of a very specific breed, don't ask me which. I think it is a Cream of Wheat Terrier. One of the rules of this breed is that it should have a people name, like Jane or Bill, etc. They chose Molly. I would have chosen Stephanie. It would immediately have a cousin in Stephan, the jade plant.

The Queen and I were all excited when we heard that Stevie and Rona were to marry in 2002. I called him to inquire what wedding date they had chosen, as we wanted to book a golf cruise around Scotland during that summer. The date wasn't set yet, but he assured me that it would not be in mid-July, which is when we were planning the cruise. We booked this once-in-a-lifetime trip, and two months later we received the invitation to their wedding.

The resultant phone call I made to Stevie started off in this fashion: "Steven, what about July 14 does not make it mid-July?" Note the use of "Steven" in this case.

Sound the alarm...
then send the cavalry home

Picture this: A burglar breaks into a home, a motion detector captures his movements, the alarm is sounded, the police dispatched, and the criminal apprehended. Is that how it really works?

The police will tell you that just knowing there is an alarm is the deterrent. That's why I wanted to buy just the sign and window decals. The Queen, however, decided that she needed the protection of an alarm system, because I might be off climbing an Alp or something.

The other thing the police will tell you is that their biggest alarm headache is the false alarm. In our town, they have a policy of charging $50 for every false alarm that they have to respond to. This is done in the hope of making people more cautious about setting off false alarms.

This story is not about the alarm company, nor the police. It's about one of my sons-in-law. I have two. Both still are under the happy illusion that they are princes to both my princesses. They haven't found out that the Queen rules, with the princesses right behind; the rest of us are serfs. It will stay that way too, until little royalty are born and they become, in like fashion, princesses or princes. My sons-in-law and I will always be serfs, plain and simple. Both of these guys are intelligent enough, but they still haven't figured this out. Ah, youth.

The serf-who-would-be-prince who is married to my youngest is a very resourceful guy. He has a number of talents. He is in advertising, which is sort of sales without traveling that much. He has one major shortcoming: namely, not knowing how to operate my alarm system. There really isn't much incentive for him to learn, as I am the one on the hook for the fifty-buck false alarm charge.

It is quite simple to stop a false alarm. Once the system is tripped, if the PIN is not entered within a certain time frame—thirty seconds or so—the alarm goes off. The alarm company then calls the house. If you give them the secret word, they turn off the alarm.

When the serf-who-would-be-prince arrived this particular day, not only did he set off the alarm and fail to enter the correct PIN, he had no idea what the secret word was. I used to have it tacked up next to the alarm, but the Queen felt that this would give the crooks an edge. "Well, only if they can read," I countered, but that didn't help. There are just too many literate crooks in this world.

When my son-in-law set off the alarm and failed the secret word test, the alarm company did what they are supposed to do. They did what they are paid to do. They called the police, who arrived very quickly.

It wouldn't have mattered anyway. My son-in-law wasn't going anywhere. Why would he? Our house is usually stocked with tons of food, wine, beer, and everything that the young royals or their serfs desire. Just the possibility of either couple visiting sets the Queen off to making shopping lists and menu plans. If by chance both princesses are scheduled to come the same weekend, you better get to the local supermarket before she does.

So there he was in food and beverage heaven, with the alarm still blazing away, when the police arrived. Now, a lot of things could have happened, some good, some bad. Here is a young guy in my house who does not know either the PIN code or the secret word. Yes, he does have a key, but he could have gotten it by devious means.

Not only did he have nothing to prove that he belonged in my house, but at that point, he was not even an official son-in-law. They were only engaged at the time, so he was actually a serf-in-training.

When the story was related to me some time later, I had dreams of him being carted off in handcuffs, with the neighbors peeking out from behind their drapes. That would show him not to forget the secret code. That would show the Queen that posting it up next to the alarm would have been a good idea. Vindication!

However, you recall my son-in-law is in advertising. One credo in advertising is "Get the graphics right." Well, actually, I don't know if it is a credo, but have you ever been convinced to buy something by an ad with bad pictures? I haven't. In fact, I have bought stuff I don't even want just because it looked good in the advert.

There they were, the police and my soon-to-be-son-in-law. He tried to explain who he was. The only "proof" that he belonged in my house was a picture of him with the family hanging in the kitchen. But how would the cops know that it was our family?

Well, there was another picture. We have a photo in the living room of my daughter with the guy she went to the prom with (not my son-in-law). A few months before, my son-in-law had pasted a head shot of himself over the other guy's face. On the outside of the glass, I might add.

The cops bought it. No handcuffs, no show for the neighbors, nothing. What I really hoped for was the come-bail-me-out telephone call, to which I was going to reply, "I never heard of this man before in my life." It would have been worth the wrath of both the Queen and his princess.

So here is the message you should take away from this story. When breaking into a house, have a collection of family pictures, but make sure you are in one. Oh, and bring a small head shot to paste over someone else's face.

The gift that keeps on giving

We are a gift-giving, card-sending family. Birthdays, anniversaries and Christmas are not the only occasions. It seems we are always planning what to get for someone. Don't get me wrong; I cherish being able to do that.

When it comes to gifts for our daughters, the Queen has elevated the giving process to an art form. Each child has a credit card in her name, and we get the bill. At first, when they were away at college, it was for emergencies. Now it is for "parental-sponsored activities," which as far as I can tell is anything that the Queen decides. Thank God, the spending limit is only $500 on these cards.

We gave each of our daughters and their husbands golf clubs for their first anniversaries. That was pretty simple and meaningful, as we enjoy golfing together.

On my oldest daughter's second anniversary, we were wondering what we could get them. The Queen has a simple rule. When you don't know, you should ask. It's sort of a feminine thing, like asking directions. So she asked what they needed. I only heard one side of the phone conversation. It went something like this.

Queen to princess number 1: "Your father and I wanted to know what you and Len want for your anniversary."

Pause, then the Queen said in astonishment: "A tent? That's what you want?"

My daughter and her husband like portaging through the Canadian wilderness, so the choice of a tent did not surprise me. I did breathe a sigh of relief. How much could a tent cost?

Queen again: "You know, your father and I were thinking that you really need a new refrigerator. How about we get a fridge instead of a tent?"

Wait a minute! For a few seconds, I was getting off with a tent—something I was sure we could get at Wall-Mart for $29.99. A fridge—where did that come from?

Wanting to keep me informed, the Queen turned to me and said, "She's going to ask Len if he wants a refrigerator for their anniversary instead of a tent."

Another pause while the Queen listened to our daughter's response. Then the Queen turned to me and proudly announced, "Len agreed on the fridge."

The Queen then continued with our daughter: "So look around and get one with all the features you want and put it on our emergencies credit card. Oh, and if it is more than the $1,500 spending limit on the card, let me know, and your father will increase it."

Three things struck me about this conversation.

One: My son-in-law is no dummy. Of course he wanted a refrigerator instead of a $29.95 Wal-Mart tent.

Two: Maybe the Queen was "thinking that you really need a new refrigerator," but I certainly wasn't. Their refrigerator seems perfectly good to me. I only drink red wine, so I don't care if their beer is warm.

And three: When did the spending limit on this card increase to $1,500?

I had very little recourse by this point. How could I renege on an offer the Queen made? Ah, well. This was the second anniversary. I was sure that all this gift giving would slow down. Of course, I did not realize that they still had an old stove—that was the third anniversary. And then they started to remodel their home, so I think I may be on the hook for a dishwasher soon.

I figured I would get off easily with the younger of the two princesses, because she moved into a more modern home, a downtown

Toronto condo that is about the size of a good walk-in closet here in Ohio, but at least all the appliances are new.

I never considered the new tires for their Volkswagen. I was going to fight that one on the grounds that they both walk to work, but I was reminded that they do use the car to travel down to see us. We wouldn't want to discourage them from visiting, would we?

Good idea. Encourage them to visit. Especially in the summertime, when we all can play golf together. With clubs I bought for them, with balls I supply, at my golf club where I pay for the rounds. Let's throw in some lessons, as well. This reminds me of that famous bumper sticker, "I'm spending my kids' inheritance." Except I would adapt the phase to read, "I'm spending my kids' inheritance—on them."

My chop saw

In thirty years of doing my own woodwork, I had often used a hand backsaw and a miter box. They had become staples of my tool collection, almost like old friends. I prided myself on being very capable with these instruments. I could work magic, whether with a piece of molding or a homemade picture frame. It is true that crown molding was always a challenge, but by the results one would have to acknowledge that I met and conquered that challenge, all with my trusty handsaw and miter box.

One pleasant day in 2001, I was walking through Sears when I spied a display of electric miter saws. I immediately thought, "One of these will be mine by the end of the day."

Usually for a purchase like this, I would investigate the features and quality from a lot of angles. I'd ask people who had one about what they liked or disliked. I would read through *Consumer Reports* for pluses and minuses. I'd ask the sales person for more details. Not today. I looked them over, made a decision, and one became mine.

Funny thing about men and tools: there is this bond. The bond usually starts even before the moment of purchase and grows with every use. I am not a car enthusiast. They are only methods of transportation to me, but the way I feel about tools must be what a real driver feels about his car. The only other thing I can liken it to in my life is golf equipment. God help the person who stands between my putter and me. This miter saw purchase was no different. I couldn't wait until I had a project to do.

Now herein lies the problem. We had moved into a brand new house. There wasn't much renovation to be done. With my travel schedule, I did not have a lot of time to start up new projects. So the new miter saw, still in its shrink wrap, came out of my trunk and rested on the floor of the garage. I got to see it every day when I pulled the car in. Wow, what fun I would have when I finally got to use it. Maybe something would rot out and have to be replaced, a windowsill or a piece of flashing—something, anything.

The saw stayed in the garage for five months, still shrink-wrapped. Occasionally the Queen would ask about why I bought that "thingamajig." I never waivered. This was to be a life-changing experience for me ... once there were wood working projects to undertake, that is.

Then the next big move happened, from the garage into the downstairs workshop. My basement workshop is quite impressive. Mostly hand tools but very functional. I have hung my assortment of tools on some twenty-four linear feet of four-foot-high pegboard. Most of these tools were acquired by me, but some were handed down from my father, and a few chisels were even handed down from my stonecutter grandfather. My workshop would be the place where my electric miter saw would work its magic.

It actually stayed shrink-wrapped for another three and a half months. Then, almost nine months after I bought it, on a rainy Saturday with not much else going on, I unpacked it and set it up. This involved putting the saw blade on and cutting a notch in the plastic base. For good measure, I even cut its first piece of wood: a knotty pine one-by-four.

Of course, I still didn't have any projects to do with it. It just sat there, but I did have an electric miter saw. I tried to work it into conversations with my male friends, playing down its newness, implying that I had it all my life. When one guy mentioned that he was about to finish his basement, I offered to lend him my saw and even to come over to demonstrate how to use it. It's a good thing that he didn't take me up on my offer, because I had still only cut one little one-by-four and couldn't really explain anything to him.

More than a full year after I bought this saw, never having turned it on for actual project work, the elder of my two princesses bought a house, an eighty-five -year-old house that needed some renovation. Correction: a lot of renovation. Their plans were rather modest in the beginning, but one thing led to another. Now, five years later, they have laid hardwood floors throughout, added on a ten-by-twelve-foot extension, completely remodeled the bathroom and kitchen, and added a garage. They did all the work themselves, from digging the foundations to the final molding.

Near the outset of the massive renovation project, the Queen realized that I had a valuable asset in my workshop that I was not using, namely the electric miter saw. She casually mentioned, "The kids could really use that thingamajig you bought and left in the garage for months."

From the beginning of their renovation plans, I was very supportive of my daughter and her husband, but this was asking a lot. After all, she and her husband love to camp and can spend weeks in the Canadian wilderness portaging back into the interior. Why do they need more than a semi-dry place to put their sleeping bags down? I was suddenly of the opinion that the house they bought looked just fine the way it was. After all, they might destroy the character of the 1930-ish bathroom. It was kind of quaint that they had to crawl under the tub to turn the hot water on before a shower. Bending was good exercise to boot. It was easier than what they had to do in the Canadian wilderness. At least at home, they had toilet paper and no need for leaves. Yes, their eighty-five-year-old house was pretty good the way it was. They didn't need any renovations, especially none that involved my miter saw.

This did not stop me thinking that they really could use my saw, though. But wait—I bought it in the USA, and they live in Canada. Maybe the metric thing would screw it up? Maybe the saw was not compatible with the blades they could get? No such luck; blades seem to fit all saws.

Okay, how about the instructions? I wouldn't feel right if I gave my Canadian daughter a saw that did not have instructions in both English and French. I'm sure there's a law in Canada against that, anyway. Why, my newly won Canadian citizenship might be revoked, all over a miter saw. I could give them $200 and they could buy their own saw, with "instructions en Français." The Queen pointed out that would be a waste of money, since my saw was sitting downstairs, idle. Besides, Sears *had* included French instructions with my saw.

It was inevitable. My electric miter saw, the one I lusted over during its five months in the garage and three and a half months downstairs, was to be inherited by my daughter and her husband before I even died.

In December 2005, two years after I had given away my miter saw, I put a wine cellar in my Ohio home. My sons-in-law helped. Actually, the one with my miter saw was the construction foreman, and he brought the saw with him. For one gleaming moment, I was able to benefit from my saw. I dared not operate it, as I was unsure if I could part with it once I actually cut a piece of wood.

My saw was happy; it had found a place where it was needed—not in the new house of a part-time handy man, but in the hands of a young couple coping with their old house and making it a home. My saw was where it should be.

Postscript: It is over a year later, and the Queen has just found a tool that my daughter left in a draw in her old room, a spoke shaver, a two-handed plane that can be used to "shape and smooth curved wood" (Stanley Tools Company description). My princess had used it to shape a canoe paddle from a larger piece of wood.

The Queen felt quite proud of herself when she presented this thing, saying, "Here, you can hang this in your shop downstairs. Take it in repayment for that thingamajig you gave the kids."

Next Christmas, canoe paddles for everyone.

You complete me

Recently I was in the doctor's office, and it became clear that I was going to be waiting for a while. The magazine rack held two items worth reading. One was a year-old *Woman's Day* magazine, and the other was a catalogue for a men's hunting and outdoor store. I took the *Woman's Day*.

My choice was partly predicated on the fact that I am a city guy and don't hunt. More importantly, the *Woman's Day* cover highlighted an article entitled *28 Ways to Say I Love You*. It was the February issue, so this pre-Valentine article made sense. I didn't want to give it too much credibility, because it was last year's magazine, and I wouldn't want to be accused of using last year's romantic advice on this year's woman.

The first item that appeared on the list of twenty-eight was called *You complete me*. It talked about looking long and hard to find something that your mate didn't get when he or she was younger. "The erector set he begged for but didn't get on his seventh birthday," it stated, or an album to fill out her collection. This was actually a pretty good idea. We all have something that was very important to us at one time that we never got. Life is like that.

I assumed that the Queen had some item that she had longed for in her younger days but never received. If I could find out what it was, I could get it for her now and "complete" her. I devised a clever plan to find out what the item was.

This clever plan involved telling her about something I had missed in my youth and then letting her give an example from her past. Then she would divulge the exact present that I should get her. Cunning, wasn't I?

There are often issues with my clever plans. This one was no different. In this case, I happened to pick an item from my past that caused me to focus on it so much that we never got to talk about what she needed to "complete" her. That was my downfall. You'll understand when I tell you about my item

Sometime in the mid 1950s, I was absolutely taken by a rubber stamp set that appeared on the back of a Kellogg's cereal box. It had thirty rubber stamps, each one with a different animal on it. I actually saved the money and sent away for it. I think it was 25 cents. I am not sure if I was old enough to address the envelope, or if I put a stamp on it. In my mind, I did send away for it.

My five-year-old mind was convinced this would be a fantastic item. I could just imagine all the things I could do with these stamps. It even had inkpads, one red and one black.

For some reason it never arrived. I waited and hoped for six months, but no stamp set. Soon it left my day-to-day thoughts, but every once in awhile, I would remember it and wonder.

Fifteen years later when I was twenty years old, we moved from that house. I do remember thinking, "We can't move! How will the people in Battle Creek ever find me to deliver the stamp set?" Okay, it was a last ditch effort to stay in my childhood home and, in a way, remain a boy forever. We moved, I never got my stamp set, and somewhere along the way, I grew up.

Oh, by the way. I finally got around to discovering what my wife missed as a child. I used another clever plan that most men don't ever consider. I simply asked her.

She explained, "My mother did not let me go to Shea Stadium to see the Beatles back in '63. I wished I had gone." As she spoke, I realized that this wasn't very useful information, since it was impossible for me to give her the experience she missed. With her next breath, I understood why we have been together for over thirty-seven years. She said, "But you fixed that when you took me to see Paul McCartney when he was in Cleveland a few years ago." Paul McCartney was her set of stamps.

I suppose that proves that if you really know and love someone, you most likely already know what will "complete" them. The answer is: you do.

Francs, lira, and more francs

The euro has made a big difference in travel. With the exception of only a few countries, UK and Switzerland being two major ones, the whole of Europe now uses a common currency. It was not always this way.

I have a good friend with whom I have traveled a fair amount who conveniently never got the currency right. My friend is a very accomplished businessperson who has traveled extensively throughout Europe. That is why he is on shaky ground when he pleads ignorance of local currency situations.

It all started in 1999 with a vacation he, his wife, my wife, and I took in Chamonix, at the base of Mont Blanc in France. Both couples are very comfortable with each other. We thoroughly enjoy each other's company. My friend especially enjoys sticking me with the bill whenever he can. It's sort of a game with him. During this trip, we hiked, took side trips to medieval towns, ate in typical French gourmet fashion, and really enjoyed ourselves.

There was only one problem. He never had any money. This was before the euro, and therefore we were dealing in various currencies. A little geography lesson is needed here. Chamonix is at the juncture of three countries, France, Switzerland, and Italy. There is a mountain pass into Switzerland and a tunnel into Italy. In 1999, the tunnel was closed because of extensive repairs needed after a rather horrific accident. To get to Italy, therefore, travelers had to take the pass into Switzerland and then another pass from Switzerland into Italy.

We were enjoying a great time when the two Queens (his wife and mine) decided that we needed an Italian meal. There are a number of good Italian restaurants in Chamonix, but our royal wives wanted a real Italian (in Italy) meal.

In those pre-euro days, I would travel with a variety of currency, so I had French francs, Italian lira, and Swiss francs. My friend had, at best, some U.S. dollars, and he may have had some pounds sterling. Like a boy scout, he was always prepared, not for the country he was in, but for a British invasion of the Alps.

Off to Italy, by way of Switzerland, we went. This was a leisurely trip, so we found ourselves stopping often for a coffee or for minor things like gasoline. Amazingly, at all of these stops, my friend never had the currency of the country we were in. In Switzerland, he had no Swiss francs, so I paid for morning coffee. In Italy, he had no lira, so I paid for lunch and some postcards. Back in Switzerland, he still had no Swiss francs, so I paid for the coffee again, plus gas. Once back in France he informed me that he was low on French francs. Therefore, I was stuck with a larger share of the dinner bill than I had expected. This guy is a pro.

This prompted Sue and I to send a postcard to his address in the USA. It was waiting for him when he got home. It simply read, "Having a good time, wish your money was here."

Guess who's coming to dinner
and staying eight months?

As you may remember, I refer to my wife of over thirty-seven years as the Queen. Like every monarch, her simple wish is to be obeyed. I have also dubbed my two daughters the princesses. It is a known fact that royalty does not just start on its own. It must be bred. So if you want to know the lineage of my wife and daughters' majesty, you need only look back one generation to my mother-in-law.

She is a down-to-earth person who, as they say, "has her head screwed on straight." Of course, it wasn't her head that gave her the medical problems that brought her to live with us for eight months. It was a combination of her heart and hip. Once the hip went out, on a gambling trip to Vegas, I might add, she could not get a replacement due to her malformed heart valve. The hospitals were afraid she wouldn't make it through the hip operation with her valve problem. I figured if she were a true gambler she would have tried it, but I guess she was more inclined to stand at the slots and ruin her hip than she was to try her luck in the operating room.

My brother-in-law lives very near my mother-in-law, but the Queen quickly decided that he would be of little assistance, since he is a man. Kind of sexist, I think, but true in this case. It was more important that the Queen assist in the Queen Moth's rehabilitation. (Her two children call her Moth, pronounced like the first syllable of the word *mother*, not like the wool-eating, flying insect. It's odd, but it's tradition.)

Since Cleveland boasts one of the best heart hospitals in the United States, it was decided that she would have the heart operation and then the hip operation at the Cleveland Clinic. She would be near her daughter and her son-in-law. I have a friend who bemoans the fact that his thirty-something kids have moved back in with him. In 2000, I had an eighty-something mother-in-law move in with us. What a way to begin the millennium.

Over the years, I have become accustomed to various looks people give me. Like the look of non-comprehension when I try to speak French, for instance. During her stay, my mother-in-law contributed a new look I hadn't seen before—the "If there was a good reason for me to let you marry my daughter, I, for the life of me, can't remember it" look.

My mother-in-law has a very interesting characteristic. She is a rule-follower. I don't mean she follows rules some of the time, or even when it is convenient; she follows rules *always*. She doesn't follow any rule-giver, however. She only follows rules given by someone with credentials, like a doctor or nurse. So when I wanted to impose the "anyone who is in my house for more than six months must sleep with a plastic bag over their head" rule, she did not follow it. Damn, I knew I should have gone to medical school.

The rule-follower in Grammy was made painfully clear to me one evening as I sat at my office desk getting ready to pack up for the day. My wife called and asked if I could bring home some Maalox. I informed her that we had substantial amounts of Mylanta under my sink. I seemed to need it more since my mother-in-law moved in. The Queen told me that she was aware of my stash of antacids, but her mother wanted Maalox.

I started to explain that they actually did the same thing, but the Queen informed me that her mom's doctor had said that if she got indigestion, she should "take some Maalox." So that was all she was going to take. I wondered out loud to my wife: "If the doctor had told her to wipe her ass with Charmin and we only had Scotts, would I need to out to the store as well?" The silence on the other end of the phone told me I was going to the store or not coming home.

We did have our fun moments. I mean besides the day she moved back to New York. One memorable instance was when Grammy was doing quite well, and Sue had assigned her some chores. One was helping us set the table. In this instance, she was bringing some coffee cups to the table. She had two cups in one hand while the other was on the walker. She would push the walker forward, take her step, then repeat. If you wanted the cups on the table by the next morning's breakfast, it would be a good idea for her to start her trek two days before, but she did quite well—never dropped a cup.

This particular time she was in the middle of her sojourn across the kitchen, holding two cups in her right hand. I just got the idea that she looked like a handicapped person begging in the street. So I took two quarters out of my pocket and dropped them in the cups. She laughed heartily. I would laugh too if someone gave me 50 cents for carrying two cups twenty feet.

Anyway, she recovered and, all kidding aside, her stay with us was not an effort at all. Funny thing, though; she's coming next month for a couple of weeks, but only after I leave for Switzerland … go figure.

My inheritance

A few years ago, my mother decided that my two sisters and I should look over what there was to inherit among her belongings and take them then. Sounds kind of morbid, but that is what she wanted. If we wouldn't take those items then, "they might be thrown out." We all knew that was an idle threat, as my mother never threw anything away. Moldy bread, she claims, makes great toast.

There are some things that just seemed to "belong" to a certain child. One of these was the soup tureen that I bought for my mother in 1970 when I was working at a department store. It is green, her favorite color, and to my recollection it never held soup. It was the centerpiece on her dining room table and was mostly used to hold expired coupons for things she really didn't need. My connection to this item runs deep, so I assumed that my sisters would not contest my claim to it. I also assumed that they secretly thought it a bit tacky. Whether the Queen would find a place for it in our home was another matter.

I am afraid it will eventually be cast into the basement next to the three-foot high statue of W. C. Fields that I inherited from my father. W. C. was his favorite comedian. I actually had the statue in my office, until my director of marketing asked why I had a statue of a man picking his nose. It was W. C. in one of his contemplative poses that indeed resembled a man picking his nose. It is now relegated to the basement.

At the time, the soup tureen was fulfilling the coupon-holding function, so I did not ask my mother for it, but there was one item that I did indeed take her up on and actually asked for. Well, I didn't exactly ask, but I did write on the back of it, "To be inherited by Gerard." She then said I should take it immediately. This was the famous Italian cheese grater. I didn't want the cheese grater to meet the same dismal demise as the slightly less famous ravioli board.

The ravioli board was a big piece of wood about four feet by four feet that was placed on the table when Grandma made ravioli. I am not sure why she and Mom didn't just wash the tabletop and use that. Instead, the cooks always went and fetched this board out of the cellar, where mice were running over it most of the time. After Grandma stopped making ravioli in her later years, it served as the base for my electric train set. It actually ended up as part of the floor in the attic of my first house. I doubt that the people who now own the home understand the heritage of that board. In any event, I didn't want the cheese grater to end up, unappreciated, in some attic.

The grater must be preserved, and I was the one to do it. Let me describe this unique object. It is made mostly of wood and looks like a box. It measures about eight inches by twelve inches (since it was made in Italy, make that twenty centimeters by thirty centimeters). The top of this box holds a typical perforated metal grating unit. Under this metal grater is a drawer into which the grated cheese falls. The draw has a white knob on it to facilitate opening and removing the cheese.

After years of use on high fat Parmesan and the occasional Romano cheeses, the wood was showing its wear. My father rebuilt the entire thing using new wood, but he retained the grater unit and the knob. So this item is not only significant on its own behalf; since my father has been gone for over thirty years, I consider the grater to be a part of him. I can see him meticulously tracing the old wood onto the new.

I don't use it to grate cheese anymore, but it hung on our wall for a number of years. It made a wonderful conversation piece. Sorry to say, when our kitchen was remodeled, it too found itself in the basement, not more than fifteen feet away from the W. C. Fields statue. I guess it will stay there until we retire and move south, where they don't have basements. Then I think it will end up in the attic. I guess the ravioli board just took a short cut.

Margaret Mary

I just got off the phone with my eldest sister. Unusually, it was a pleasant conversation for both of us. Yes, it is unusual for both of us to have a pleasant conversation together. In my opinion, all our conversation are pleasant for her but not often for me. That sounds egotistical, but I will admit that my lack of patience with my sister is *my* problem. It's funny, because I seem to have infinite patience with many other people. Ah, family.

My sister is a very intelligent woman. She really is a groundbreaker, as all well-educated women born right after the war are. They are the first generation who started to gain the equality so badly needed in our society. Things are not perfect now, but in North America at least, the next generation had a much better starting point. Don't get me wrong—she is not really a feminist. I don't think she ever burned her bra, unless she ironed it once on the wrong setting. (She irons everything. It wouldn't surprise me if she did iron her bra.) She is more of an everyday woman going about her job with great dedication and little pay, making it all work and making a difference in people's lives.

How could I have an unpleasant conversation with her? There are two reasons. One is simply that she is my sister. She is the oldest. I am the youngest. Three and a half years separate us. The second reason is, she is a *teacher*.

My sister's job is teaching math to high school students in a Catholic high school in the Bronx. In addition, she is a *teacher*. Anna Quindlen wrote in her delightful *A Short Guide to a Happy Life*, "Don't ever confuse the two, your life and your work." My sister understands this. In the depths of her soul, she also happens to be a *teacher*. Her life goal, not just her professional goal, is to teach. I am not sure I have ever met someone as perfectly suited for his or her job. Therein lies the problem between us.

A teacher wants you to understand everything about a subject, down to the minute details. Although that is what her students in linear geometry may want and need, I don't particularly need to know all about the subject of her weekend. God forbid I give her an opening like, "How was the dinner last week?" I better get a pen if I do, because she will be giving me the recipes shortly. A good friend of mine in Canada has a saying about people like this: "Ask them the time, and they'll tell you how to build a watch." That's my sister Margaret Mary.

Case in point: Our mother was recovering from a broken hip in a rehab center in late 2005. I had tried to call Mom but didn't get an answer, which is surprising for someone laid up in her bed. Ah ha. I finally remember something about her number being changed, so I called my sister to get the new phone number. The conversation went something like this:

Me: "Hello, Margaret, how are you?"

MM: "Fine, and Mom's doing fine as well."

Me: "That's why I'm calling. I can't seem to get in touch. Did they change her number?"

MM: "Oh, yes. You know the lady who was in the bed by the window? She left the center. Laura and I were thinking that it would be good if Mom had the bed near the window, so we requested she be moved, and with that she got a new phone number."

Me: "Okay, good. What's her number?"

MM: "I don't know why they let that lady out already, but I guess she was ready to go home. Remember, this is the lady whose daughter came in every day and brought her meals. Boy, some of that food was quite good. Well, actually I only got to smell it. Even though she always offered Mom a taste, Mom thought it was odd. You know that meant it wasn't Italian (laugh). But they released her anyway. She was very nice. I think she lived in Dobbs Ferry or someplace like that …"

Me (interrupting): "Margaret. I want to call Mom before it's too late. Can you give me the number?"

MM: "Oh, Gerard, she's up to all hours. You know, someone at the home asked me if this was true since the accident, but I had to admit she was always a night owl, even when we were young. I wondered if that was because Daddy worked such odd hours at the newspaper. I actually asked her once, and she said that even before they were married she was a night owl."

Me (raising my voice): "Listen, I don't want to hear the history of the lady in the next bed, nor why Mom goes to bed at 2 AM. Just give me the number."

In my defense, mine was the frustration of a son far away from a sick parent. Or maybe not, but I'm sticking to that story.

You should have seen the look I got from the Queen. She was listening to half of the conversation, but she still took my sister's side. "Don't talk to your sister like that," she said with a menacing stare. I mumbled something, wrote down the number, continued to talk to my sister for a few minutes, then hung up and called Mom.

To be honest, if I were Mary Margaret, I wouldn't put up with my rudeness in cutting her off. However, in a world where everyone seems to want to change everyone else, she gets it. She understands me, she understands who we both are, and that it is okay for each of us to be us ... she the *teacher,* me the impatient brother.

This past Christmas, when I opened my present from her, it all made sense. It was a pillow with an inscription on it that read: "I smile because you are my brother. I laugh because there's nothing you can do about it."

So what's the truth about Saint Joey?

Today happens to be my brother-in-law's birthday. So I'll write about him. He is the husband of my oldest sister, and as the title of this piece implies, he has the patience of a saint.

Joey, or Joe, grew up in our neighborhood. Well, that's not exactly true, since he actually grew up in Queens: a minor borough. We grew up in the Bronx, which, as you may know, is the only borough in New York City that is on the mainland of the United States; all the rest are island republics.

Joe is of English-Irish heritage. That's not at completely true either, since he is 100 percent Sicilian. He even has family over there. His surname has five syllables and is more of a challenge to pronounce than ours is. Since it starts with a *G,* it is at least closer to the front of the alphabet.

Joe is a modern renaissance man who enjoys both rap music and opera. Okay, so that's really a lie. He likes the "do-wop" music of the fifties and, come to think of it, he may be permanently stuck in that decade. He gets a sort of glazed look in his eyes when you mention Eisenhower, sock hops, and the Four Seasons.

Joe is a cosmopolitan guy who likes to travel around the world and is as much at home in Shanghai as he is in Brooklyn. That's a lie too. He visited us in England once, and upon seeing the levers we had on our doors, he asked, "Why don't they use door knobs like the rest of the world?" ("Rest of the world" translates to "Queens, the Bronx, and Yonkers.")

I went to breakfast with Joe yesterday, to celebrate his birthday. I was visiting him in upstate New York where they live. Well, actually that's not true, since they live in Yonkers, a few miles north of the New York City border. To a Bronx boy, however, Yonkers is upstate. To Joe, who hails from Queens, it is just south of the Arctic. By his reckoning, my cousins from Plattsburgh must reside at the North Pole.

When Joe entered the family, we got a great sense of humor, a nice guy, and, most importantly, a fellow who goes very well with my sister. He had a big effect on me. His outgoing personality became a model for me when I was in my formative adolescent years. He may be one reason for my success in later life.

Joe seems almost perfect. His only flaw may be that he likes to vacuum the house while dressed in his pajamas, which he often puts on at about 7 PM … and that's the truth.

A funny thing happened on the way to Cincinnati

In late August 2005, I was on my way to Cincinnati by car on I-71, heading for a lunch meeting there. I live in a Cleveland suburb, so the journey takes four hours, with Columbus being halfway. Just outside of Columbus, I received a call informing me that my meeting was changed to later in the afternoon. No problem; I could continue into the office and spend some time answering my e-mails.

But wait! Maybe I could stop in to see if my high school girlfriend was home. Little chance, I thought, as she and her husband both work. She has lived in Columbus for ten years, and I haven't seen her since the 25th high school reunion, twelve years ago. I haven't seen her husband in at least twenty years.

Using the GPS, I discovered that their home was just a few miles off Route 71. Between the GPS and the cell phone, it seemed as if technology was urging me to drop in. Okay, so they might not be home in the middle of the day, but what a surprise they would get when they saw my card in their door. What do you expect me to do: drive up to the house, look at it, ring the bell, and then just leave? My cousin Howie, the policeman, had a word for that—stalking.

There I was, on Cris and Joanne's street (notice the use of "Cris and Joanne" rather than "Joanne and Cris"—I've learned from Howie). Well, what to my wondering eyes did appear but their house, with the garage door open. There, just inside the garage, was a person who looked like a "slightly older than last time I saw him" Cris. He was kneeling down working on some sort of chore. What luck! At least I would get to see my old girlfriend's husband. (There is something intrinsically wrong with that remark, but I'll leave it in to keep my word count up.)

As I pulled into the driveway, this person, who indeed did turn out to be Cris, looked up with what I can only say was total disgust on his face. He threw down the tool he had in his hand and menacingly walked toward my car. Thoughts flashed through my head. Why be mad at me? I hadn't seen him in years. Did he even know it was me in this car (very doubtful)? Maybe he hated people in red GM cars?

As I opened the door, I heard him say, "You just drove over wet cement!" How did I know he had just finished patching his driveway? This was some way to renew a friendship after all these years.

In hindsight, I think that I had options. Since I was now sure he did not recognize me, I could have easily asked if this was the "Williams" house (not their name), apologized, and headed off. But no, I was on a mission to renew old friendships, not exactly by first destroying the guy's property, but it was a start.

I apologized, then asked, "Are you Cris?" After the affirmative answer, I said, "You probably don't remember me ..." He interrupted and said, "Of course I do. You're Gerry Tortorelli." That made me feel good, even though he admitted it was the Bronx accent that gave me away.

After he had smoothed out the offended cement, we had a delightful half-hour chat over a cool drink. Returning to the driveway, we realized that my car was still on the wrong side of the wet cement. Cris suggested that I drive out over the lawn, but I knew what game he was playing. Just imagine when Joanne returned home that evening; he would say, "Your old boyfriend was here, and not only did he wreck my cement; he also ruined the lawn."

So, gingerly I backed up over the almost dry concrete and was on my way, knowing at least that I made an impression ... in his driveway.

Postscript: This is the first story I actually finished for this book. As we got near to publishing, I wanted to put the stories into a time frame, so I consulted my electronic calendar. I realized that the day the Cincinnati meeting was delayed and I ended up driving over their wet cement was August 23, 2005, Joanne and Cris's thirty-sixth wedding anniversary. What are old boyfriends for, anyway?

Brian is...

I have a nephew. His name is Brian. He is the only son of my wife's brother and his wife. I can use many words to describe him, but the one that comes to mind is *unique.* I know everyone is unique but *Brian is Brian.*

Brian visits us in Ohio most years for a week or so. Once while he was here, he chatted with the waiter at the local Bob Evans restaurant where he buys me breakfast. The waiter's name was Joe. Whenever he talked to me over the following year, he would ask how Joe was. *Brian is very friendly.*

We usually have outings and projects planned when he visits. An outing could be something as simple as going to breakfast every day, and a project might be power-washing my driveway. He always seems to enjoy these activities, and indeed, he usually asks about two months before he arrives what the activity schedule will be. *Brian likes schedules.*

Some young people don't have time for the older folks. Brian enjoys time with both of his eighty-plus-year-old grandmothers and looks forward to coming home to see them. He has time for all the cousins, aunts, and uncles. *Brian has a great sense of family.*

I can understand why he likes his uncles—especially me—I treat him so well. Okay, so that's not exactly true. In fact, I do take advantage of his good nature from time to time. We established a tradition a few years ago that he would buy breakfast for both of us on all the days that end in *y*. He agreed before he realized that all days end in *y*. Hey, a deal is a deal. *Brian honors his commitments.*

Brian inherited his love of cleanliness from his mother. I think that's nice, except on the occasions when it annoys me, which, by the way, is all days that end in *y*. One time we were in the middle of the "making lasagna project," when I happened to get a few drops of the white sauce on the counter. He said, "Uncle G, there's a mess here, can you clean it up?" I said something like, "We'll get that later." After Brian reminded me for the fifth time that I had to clean up the mess, I poured about half of the ricotta, milk, and egg mixture onto the counter and said, "Now we have a real mess, and we are going to leave it there until we finish." This did get his attention, and he gave me a look that was indescribable. *Brian is a neatnik.*

He is not very athletic. He will even admit that, but he always likes to accompany me on the golf course. I have had him as a caddy on occasion, not to carry the clubs but to drive the cart and assist me. He is very good at handing me my clubs, keeping them clean, manning the pin, and not laughing when I hit a bad shot. Of course, in the beginning he would say stuff like; "Hey Uncle G, why did you hit that one into the woods?" Honesty is something you don't want in a caddy sometimes. *Brian is very honest.*

He especially likes to drive the power cart. Well, actually, he likes to drive it now, but in the beginning, I think it intimidated him. This was partly my fault, because I never gave him any instruction before his first try. The result was an altercation with a tree. He had the right idea—push on the brake, but golf cart brakes need a bit more push than other type of vehicles. As he passed by me with his foot on the brake saying in a rather desperate voice, "Uncle G, why isn't it stopping?" I could only stand there with my mouth open. Then he hit the poor maple head on. Until we got new carts the following year, cart number sixteen at Chagrin Valley Country Club had a dent in the front bumper. *Brian leaves his mark wherever he goes.*

Like all young people, he listens to music. He not only listens—he feels the music. His specialty is Broadway show music. He has seen all … let me say that again … *all* the musicals on Broadway in the last seven years. I don't think he has a T-shirt that isn't from one of the shows. He remembers them all, and he can sing most of the major parts. *Brian is musically talented.*

He lives in Connecticut now and is a greeter at a Wal-Mart store. He has been nominated for Associate of the Month a few times, and he won that honor recently. He takes a personal interest in all the shoppers he greets. As a result, customers have written glowing letters and made numerous comments to management about him. He brightens their day. *Brian has a positive effect on everyone he meets.*

Some say that people like Brian are *special.* Indeed everyone is special, but Brian, he is *unique.* He has added so much to the family that I cannot imagine our family without him. I know I miss him the years he doesn't come to Ohio. Hey, he buys me breakfast, but only on days that end in *y.*

Mawiage

Both of my daughters, born in the late 1970s, were of an impressionable age when the movie *The Princess Bride* was released. So impressionable, in fact, that a new word entered our family vocabulary: *mawiage.*

In the movie, the minister who performed Buttercup's wedding ceremony to the evil prince could not pronounce the word "marriage." He pronounced the double *r* as *w,* hence *mawiage.*

I am not sure why this stuck, but it did, and every so often one of my daughters will say "mawiage" instead of the proper word. This is done with full cognitive intent and not as an error. It is a great movie. It has characters, a twist of fate, mistaken identity, and even a giant: André, to be exact. In the end, true love wins out, or as Billy Crystal's character says, "to blathe." As we would say in the Bronx, "Ya gotta see the movie."

Sorry to say not all marriages are written so that true love wins out. Sue and I have maintained that the most important decision people make is who will be their life partner. We are very happy that both of our daughters chose whom they did. But really, us being happy is not that important. They need to be happy and confident with their decision.

Over the years, our views on successful marriage have not changed; we have just found different ways of expressing the same truth.

In the first few years, we used to say: "You have to love each other and like each other." In our own case, Sue and I are blessed because we can both say we married our best friend.

Later, we realized that it was important to like each other's families. This may not be critical for those who are not close to family, but for us it is crucial. It is so much easier when everyone gets along.

We moved to another realization once the kids came along. Kids make a strong marriage stronger. I think they do the reverse to a weak marriage, but generalizations are hard to make about something so complicated.

So there I was, with almost thirty-five years of marriage behind me, thinking I had it all figured out. The formula for marriage success was: Love each other, like each other, like each other's families, and love the kids. Life is funny. Just when you feel comfortable, some nuance comes along that contributes a new shade to the overall picture. This time it happened to be contained in a book I read last week.

One of the characters says something profound. I paraphrase what the character writes in a letter to her son on his wedding day. *Love your spouse, love your children, and love your marriage.*

Love your marriage. It involves the memories of the sharing, the pain, the lessons co-learned—in short, the life you have lived together. Embrace it, remember it, and love it.

I never thought of it that way. Funny, if someone asks me about a good friend, I'll think of the times we shared together, whether yesterday or forty years ago. It will make me smile. When thinking about my spouse, however, I usually think of Sue now, not then.

So now I have a new recipe for marriage: Love and like your spouse, love your kids, it helps to like your in-laws, and cherish your marriage itself. Oh, and marry your best friend.

That's all there is to mawiage, no matter how you pronounce it.

NY, NY: The 2006 version

I was more than a little surprised last month when I read a magazine article stating that New York was the most polite city of the thirty-five cities rated in a global study. By chance, I have lived in the top three cities. Besides New York, they are Zürich (second place) and Toronto (third). On my own scale, Toronto would be first, with Zürich a lot further back, unless, as the study authors may have done, you confuse coldness with being polite. But New York?

When asked about the results of the survey, former New York mayor Ed Koch commented, "After 9/11, New Yorkers are more caring. They understand the shortness of life." Maybe that is the case after all. I am a New Yorker, by birth and by accent. Although I visit the surrounding area often, I last lived in the immediate metropolitan area in 1972. Admittedly, my frame of reference is a bit out of date. I didn't realize how out of date until this last weekend, when my youngest princess took part in the New York City Marathon.

With two Toronto Marathons under her belt, my daughter Lynne applied and was accepted to run in the 2006 New York version of this twenty-six-mile race. The size of the event is simply staggering. Ninety thousand runners apply, thirty-seven thousand runners participate, and over two million on-lookers participate from the sidelines. I call the on-lookers "participants," because without them this would not be the New York Marathon. Some runner friends tell me that you take part in this event not for a great completion time, but for the experience.

My sister, son-in-law, wife, a cousin, and I all decided that we would "subway hop" in order to see Lynne at various points. Our intention was to catch her at mile four, mile eight, mile fourteen, mile twenty, and mile twenty-four. Although we got to those locations, we missed her twice. At mile fourteen, we missed her because we were a bit late and she had already passed. At mile four however, we were there but missed her because of the sheer number of people. That's how many people are involved.

As you can see, we did a lot of moving around. Granted, Lynne was using a bit more energy than we were, but we saw the subway, which in itself is a treat. The Queen researched it and told me that we could buy a day pass for seven dollars, which would give us unlimited use of the subway for the entire day. She thought that was a good deal. This confused me, as the last time I took the subway the tokens had that cute cut out *Y* in the middle and they cost 15 cents per ride. At that rate, our breakeven point would be forty-seven trips! The actual fare in 2006 is $2.00 per trip. I guess I am out of date a bit.

Other things about the subway have changed as well. The old urine smell is not as prevalent as I remember, and it is much cleaner from a trash point of view. Now you can actually hear the announcements on the trains. I used to tell friends that the typical New York accent came from listening to the garbled announcements on the subways. Today you can hear what they are saying, and—get this,—they apologized over the loudspeaker that the express was not running that day!

The people seemed to have changed as well. The riders have iPods galore, and yes, they are polite. I saw a number of cases of young riders offering seats to older riders. Maybe that survey was right.

Most marathon runners make sure they have their name prominently displayed somewhere on their outfit. The onlookers cheer them along using their name or anything else they can. If there are runners from another country, state, or city and they identify that, the crowd will yell encouraging remarks to them. When I saw the Swiss white cross on runners, I would use the Swiss football team slogan and yell "Hoop Suisse;" I was elated when the runners responded with a wave or a smile.

We had a large Canadian flag with us, as my daughter lives and runs out of Canada. At points, some runners would acknowledge the flag and yell, "Go, Canada." Hold on, weren't we supposed to be cheering them on? It's a strange thing, this brother and sisterhood of runners and spectators.

I was fascinated that many of the onlookers knew no one personally involved in the race. They were there cheering on strangers. As a runner, you have to be careful. One told me that he started out too quickly the first time he ran New York because the cheering got his adrenaline up. Lynne said she almost sprinted the last mile because of this effect. It really is intoxicating.

During the entire day, we saw only supportive, friendly people. They were happy to be there and happy to support the people running. They were helpful to us "foreigners" and just simply nice. My sister summed it up at the end of the weekend with a simple: "This was New York at its finest."

My runner friend Stevie explained all this to me a number of years ago. I didn't get it at the time. I don't think anyone can really understand what an event like this is without taking part. I'll have to show him this article. I know him well enough to expect that he may say, "See, I told you so," but that wouldn't be very nice. He lives in the New York area, so maybe he's more polite now too.

The Urban Legend

During my first month back in the United States after being promoted to run the North American part of our company, my assistant came to me and said she would be late the following day because of a funeral she had to attend. The deceased was not a very close relative but someone close enough that she wanted to attend the services. I offered my condolences and asked politely how she was doing with this loss. She answered matter-of-factly, "Well, he was the most miserable SOB you ever wanted to know." That direct candor and simple "Here I am, take it or leave it" attitude sums up my assistant Carol.

Being the assistant to the president gave Carol a rather strong position in the company: one that she used very well. Some days, I wondered who actually ran the place.

Carol is not a small woman, height-wise, and she can be intimidating sometimes. I had hired a director for a special project who also used Carol's services. He was a fair bit shorter and slighter than Carol. While she was helping him prepare for a meeting and the corresponding presentation, it seemed that he constantly changed his mind. This resulted in a lot of duplicate work for Carol. At one point, as he approached her with yet another change, she calmly but sternly stared down at him and said, "I can hurt you, you know." He turned around and went back into his office.

In another episode, the parent company sent us a guy to assist when we needed some furniture moved. He was a rather thin, meek, timid fellow. He was still trying to determine what to do when Carol took control and just pushed the stuff around herself. This caused him to exclaim, "You are the strongest woman I have ever seen!" He was probably right. Her strength came from weathering hardships over the course of an interesting lifetime.

One of Carol's passions is bowling. I was thinking about interjecting a funny comment about bowling being a passion, but I am sure she would retort with something about curling, so I will not go there: With Carol, discretion is the better part of valor.

One day she explained that after she bowls, sometimes her feet hurt. She then added, "I guess I should expect that, since my shoes are at least one size too small." This is the type of comment you cannot just leave unquestioned, so I asked, and she explained that she has been wearing the same bowling shoes since 1959 (this was 2001). Her Christmas present from me that year was bowling shoes, in the right size.

For some reason, one mid-October I decided to go around our U.S. headquarters wishing people a happy Canadian Thanksgiving. Carol said she knew a place to rent a pilgrim's hat. All went well, and our U.S. group finally figured out why they couldn't reach anybody in Toronto that day.

The next day, as usual, I asked Carol how her evening had been, and she explained she had spent it in jail. In returning the hat, she went through a stop sign and was stopped by the police. Upon checking her license, it was found that it had been suspended for leaving the scene of an accident two years before, which was startling since she had renewed her license since then. The cops insisted on handcuffing her. She had to call her daughter to get her out of jail. I told her the next time to call me, since I would have enjoyed seeing her being lectured by the police. She then told me what she said to the police, and I am not sure why she isn't still in jail.

Interesting things always seem to happen to Carol. I kept on telling her that she should write a book. At one point, I started to give her some ideas for chapter titles. I even kept a list in my desk draw. There was *The kleptomaniac among us*: a chapter about her first roommates who always seemed to have great things despite their low-wage jobs. *I dated a Mafia goon*: about an old "connected" boyfriend. *The cool cat*: about her keeping her dead cat in the freezer until she had time to bury it. And of course, *Auditioning for the Band,* but if I tell that story, this book would be X-rated.

Don't get me wrong, we did a lot of good work, and the company flourished. Besides the day-to-day things that any exec assistant does, Carol organized and pulled off some incredible meetings. The one that best exemplifies her skills was held at Cornell University. We were a food ingredient company, and Cornell offered a great venue based on its very strong food science department and its location about halfway between our two major facilities.

The meeting was called *Back to School* and included classes on everything from team building to the kosher status in food. We had labs, which required each group to produce their own products from scratch using the Cornell pilot lab. These were then served at graduation. Everyone stayed in the dorms and traveled by bus. Three to five classes were going on at a time. Carol did all the organization.

I have been blessed in my career with having a number of outstanding admin assistants. Whether in Switzerland, Canada, or the United States, somehow I always got great ones. In many cases, their responsibilities stretched far beyond those of admininstrative assistance. One became head of communications for our small firm and did a great job. Another ended up doing most of our marketing activity. And one, named Carol, who retired after the company was sold, became a legend. Her full name is Carol Urban, the Urban Legend. Oh, and she could hurt you, except she wouldn't. I'm almost sure she wouldn't.

The night the bitches danced

One of the hardest things I had to do in my professional career was to be part of the sale of the division I was running. Our Swiss parent company, the largest food company in the world, had decided to divest our flavor and ingredient business. We were not a mainstay for them, and since we were profitable, they could get a good price for our division. Indeed, they had chosen to sell us off to a leader in the flavor industry, another Swiss-based company, for a great price.

It was difficult for me, partly because I had a sense of ownership in this division that I had helped build into the largest savory flavor company in the world. I had worked on it on three continents and from many different positions, from flavor research to management. The worst aspect, however, was what I knew the sale would do to our employees in North America. Since the sale was already agreed to by the time I was informed of it, I could do nothing but try to ensure the best outcome for all.

We all knew it was going to be tough on my employees in North America, as the company cultures and locations probably meant few of our staff would be offered jobs in the new entity. We held a number of employee meetings between when the announcement occurred and the sale was finalized.

One of the more memorable meetings occurred when the worldwide head of the company came to our North American headquarters in Ohio. He is a German who, although he had substantial international experience, always seemed to have issues when he spoke in North America. His English was good, but sometimes he stated things the wrong way.

I was therefore worried that he might say something inappropriate by North American standards. My concern was heightened by the highly emotional state many of the employees were in because they were fearful for their jobs. It was important, however, for our employees to have access to the top guy.

So there we were, at the front of the conference room, he and I, side by side, facing the sixty or so employees who were assembled from our sales staff and headquarters staff. From my vantage point, I had a good head-on view of all the attendees. My HR director was in the front row. He was noting any follow-up issues.

Questions were asked, and it was clear there was a lot of concern in people's minds. About halfway through, a seemingly simple question was asked by one of our long-time employees. He said, "When do we become employees of the new company?"

My German boss answered, "When you go home on the night of April 30, you will be employees of our company. When you come to work on May first, you will be employees of the new company." That would have been sufficient to answer the question, but he added; "You know, the night the bitches dance."

There was an audible "Huh?" from the audience, and I turned in amazement and asked him, "What?"

He said matter-of-factly, "The night the bitches dance." He could now see the look on my face and had heard the reaction of the room, so he said in German, "Hexen," the German word for witch.

My response was "Oh, the night the witches dance."

He retorted in a voice all could hear: "Then what is a bitch?"

I said, "I'll tell you later."

The crowd erupted in laughter. It was a welcome break in the intensity of the event.

In Germany, *Walpurgisnacht*, the night between April 30 and May 1, is the night when the witches hold a large celebration on the *Blocksberg* and await the arrival of spring. It is called *the night the witches dance*.

The mistake was an innocent one that actually lightened the mood. I do believe, however, that it showed how little the Europeans understood of our side of the pond. American businessmen are often criticized for not understanding the culture or language of the countries they want to do business in. Many times this is a justifiable criticism. We should always remember it goes both ways.

7. Back and forth: One hell of a commute

After our parent company, Nestlé, sold the division I was running, I took a job with the company that bought it. They wanted someone to handle the relationship between two giants: the largest food company in the world and the largest flavor company in the world.

Since both are Swiss companies, it was obvious that I would work out of Switzerland again. Since I did not want to relocate again, I commuted from my home in Solon, Ohio, to my office north of Zürich.

I learned the names of many of the flight attendants on Zürich flights CO79 and CO80. I improved my Swiss-German somewhat. And, most importantly, I again observed firsthand the difference and similarities of people on different sides of the ocean.

An E-mail from Europe

Dear friends and family:

In the old days, about six weeks ago, they let me keep my computer password forever. Then some chip-head (translate "IS guy") decided that one month was all a password was good for. That is a problem, as all my passwords are the same and have been forever. Last month I changed my password from "Susan0703" to "Beth1129." For those who can't decipher codes, "Susan 0703" is my wife's name and her birthday, while "Beth 1129" is my daughter's name and birthday; Susan being the Queen and Beth the older princess.

There is a benefit to this, I might add. It forces you to think of a loved one while signing on to your computer. However, with some of the recent sign-on problems I have had, having to type the password every three minutes results in a major disdain for November 29.

No problem, you say; now that a new month is upon us, I can easily change the password to a Lynne password, Lynne being the younger of my two princesses. If my sign-on problems continue, I would, in like fashion, get to detest April 25. That is sort of what I was thinking.

Earlier today, I changed my main password to "Lynne425". What could be simpler? You forget one small item. There were no *y*'s or *z*'s in either "Susan0722" or "Beth1129," but, lo and behold, there is a *y* in Lynne. The German key board I am using right now has the *Y* key where the North American keyboard has the *Z* key and the *Z* key where the *Y* key should be. Today alone, I have spelled my younger daughter's name "Lznne" about twenty times. If this computer is so smart, how come it didn't know I wanted to type "Lynne"?

Why not change only a few letters, you wonder. Maybe use "Susan0722" (our anniversary) or "Beth0901" (her anniversary). The chip-heads think that is a sin. It seems you must change every letter in the password. I even think that I am breaking the rules by having two "daughter" passwords in consecutive months. I'm sure this is somehow not allowed, but if they ask, I'll say Lynne is my third cousin once removed.

In any event, I will struggle through this challenge. I am not sure what I will do next month when I run out of wives and daughters, come to think of it.

I have over 782 Tortorellis, Baiettis, Ruddys, and Heimbergers on my family tree, so I should be fine until about the year 2071.

All the best from Europe.

Oh, and by the way, if you didn't get this e-mail, it's because I couldn't sign on.

Stay well.

Love always,
Me

Curling stones and blue bras (contains nudity)

In March of 2005, the Queen and I were joined by two close friends on a curling trip to Switzerland. We signed up for two *Bonspiels*, the curling term for tournament.

In order to keep our Ohio-based curling club informed of our progress, I published reports from the field and e-mailed them back to the club. These articles were entitled *The Sojourn of the Dedolphs and Tortorellis Among the Helvetians.*[5]

The following is adapted from one of these reports…

This report is not about language, names, or, for that matter, curling. It is about dissension on the team. I will chronicle our fabulous win of Friday morning and our disappointing defeat of Friday afternoon in a later report. Now it is time to address the difficult and sensitive subject of team dynamics.

It all started with the dressing room. As one of the first teams to arrive, we choose a dressing room and proceeded to change our shoes. When we asked the organizer which dressing room was for men and which was the women's, we received one of those stares that seemed to indicate he had no idea what we

---

5   Helvetians = ancient Swiss tribe

were talking about. I get those stares whenever I try to speak French, so I know them very well. His advice: Just pick one.

As others arrived, we soon realized that dressing rooms were not separated by gender. Well, who really cares; we were only changing shoes. Others joined us in the dressing room, and we greeted them with a hearty "Bonjour."

We then played our game (winning handily, I might add). As we were walking back to the dressing room, the Queen wondered out loud if we would see the same type of things in the dressing room as before the game. I had no idea what she was talking about. She informed me that one of the women actually changed her shirt and stood there in a light blue bra for a few minutes.

Although I think I have European ideas, this shocked me. When I say shocked, I don't mean in the prudish sense of the word. I was shocked that there was a half-naked woman about ten feet away and I never noticed. (This would have been a good time to say to the Queen that I only have eyes for her naked body, but I wasn't thinking quickly enough.)

Knowing that we had at least three more games to play, it dawned on me that I could have ample opportunity to see additional sights of this sort. But what would happen if I missed them again? "We" came up with an idea. If anyone on the team saw any nakedness, they were to say the word *schnell*. This became our official nudity alert word. Schnell, German for fast, is what our fearless skip[6] had taken to yelling as a sweep call[7] during the previous week's bonspiel in the German part of Switzerland.

In the second game, we decided to give the opposition every chance to win, and they did. The Raclette party was taking place immediately after the game, so the dressing room was crammed with bodies. In a fifteen-by-fifteen room, there were about twelve of us. I went about my shoe changing without hearing a single "schnell": not a peep from anyone on my team.

---

6   skip: a curling term. The leader of the team who decides the strategy and when to sweep the rock

7   sweep call: a curling term. What the skip yells to tell the sweepers to sweep hard

Once out of the dressing room, our lead[8] commented, "Well, wasn't that interesting … the lady in the dark blue panties?"

Unless she has x-ray vision, this meant that there was again a semi-naked lady in our changing room whom I did not see. Everyone else had noticed, but not me. Hey, what happened to our nudity alert word? My team had let me down. They contended that an American team saying a German word in a French bonspiel would be a bit odd. The Queen also added that the nudity alert word wasn't the team's idea anyway. It was mine, and she wasn't going to embarrass herself just so I could look at naked Europeans.

"We" then agreed on a new nudity alert word, *Mayfield*. (This is the name of our curling club in Ohio.) If any of us heard that word, it was time to look around—there was probably some naked Swiss in the area.

My hopes rose and were dashed again when our lead yelled "Mayfield" during the preparation for the third game. It turned out to be her husband changing his shirt. I maintain that this was a misuse of the nudity alert word, but the rest of the team felt it was within the definition I had established.

By the way, I thought it was interesting that both the women's undergarments that I never saw were blue—different shades, I was told, but both blue. Blue women's underwear must have been in vogue in Switzerland in 2005.

We are going back to the same Bonspiels in 2006, and although it pains me, I have decided to keep my eyes open in the changing rooms. Of course this is just to see what color is in fashion in 2006.

Honestly, that's the only reason.

Postscript: The following year we took part in the same two Bonspiels with another couple. In the French-speaking part, we again ran into bras and assorted panties in the change room (some blue, by the way). But we had an addition. One of the players from Geneva changed his pants after the game. Evidently he needed to change his underwear as well. When told this by our lead, who is a nurse, I asked if

---

8   lead: a curling term for the person who throws the first rock

she "saw anything." Her answer: "Well, I can tell you, he's not Jewish." Ah, the Swiss.

The 99 steps

I am a creature of habit. I like my routines. To catch my normal Continental flight home for my commute back to Ohio, I take a taxi from the office at 8:30 AM, arriving at Zürich airport about an hour and a half before takeoff. I took the same taxi today, even though takeoff is an hour later due to the difference in timing between Europe and North America at the start of daylight savings time. This leaves me with an extra hour to use before takeoff.

During my extra hour, I attended a Scotch-tasting at the duty free, even though I don't drink it normally. I looked at all the tourist hats and T-shirts, and I checked up on the Swiss compulsion for exactness.

In my twenty-five years of living in or traveling to Switzerland, for the first time I found a chink in the Swiss armor of exactness. During the three years I commuted to work using the Swiss trains, once, and only once, was a Swiss train late. By four minutes, mind you, but it was late. That is Switzerland.

It doesn't stop with the trains. If a service technician is going to call on your home, he informs you of the exact time of his visit. In North America, the phone company may commit to "a time between 1 PM and 5 PM." Not the Swiss. If they tell you they will be there at 2:15, they will be there. That is the culture: clean, exact, and on time.

I fear the entire Swiss culture could be floundering, however, after what I saw this morning at the airport. In their defense, it had to do with an American fast food restaurant. The issue was with Burger King.

It actually had nothing to do with the food or the eating experience. It had to do with their new advertisement. A ten-foot high sign in the main terminal reads "Burger King 99 steps," with an arrow showing you the direction.

What tipped me off was the fact that two signs located quite a distance apart were worded with the same "99 steps." The geometry of the situation would not allow both to be correct. I had to know. With my extra hour this morning, I decided to pace off the steps to see if the Swiss were right. This is something that most Swiss would never do. Not because they are not dedicated to exactness—they are—but because they expect everything in Switzerland to be exact in the first place. If it says ninety-nine steps to BK, it *is* ninety-nine steps. I wasn't so sure.

Had the Queen been with me, she would have mumbled something about the obsessive-compulsive nature of what I was doing. The beauty was that I was alone. Don't get me wrong; I love traveling with the Queen. In cases like this, however, it does cramp my style a little.

So there I was walking and counting. Fifty-five steps got me to the large TV monitors that show the flight information. Seventy-five got me almost to the corner where the Swiss Heimwerk store is. Ninety-nine got me to … the middle of the corridor. Yes, I could see the BK, but I was still a ways away. Forty-three steps more were required for me to get to the BK entrance. One could argue that the step count should have been to the counter and not the entrance, but that would be a little picky.

That is a 43 percent error—unacceptable. That's like saying a Swiss train would leave twenty-five minutes late (43 percent of an hour), which has most likely never happened since 1291 when the country was founded. What is happening to this country? William Tell must be turning over in his grave. His son would really be unhappy knowing that exactness is not the Swiss staple any longer. Hey, when Dad is trying to shoot an apple off your head, exactness counts. The Queen would most likely argue that the number of steps it takes to get to a restaurant is insignificant. But it's the principle.

While I am discussing the shortcomings of Zürich airport, I have a bone to pick with them. The gates that are used for U.S.-bound flights are in the E concourse. There is an unmanned train that takes you to the E concourse from the main building. It runs like those Disney trains, on some type of computer system. My issue is this: For a train that only makes two stops, it spends about a third of its time empty. Once it arrives at one of the stops, all passengers are asked to exit, and no one is allowed to board. The empty train then travels into a dead-end tunnel where it reverses direction and travels back on the other track heading in the opposite way.

It takes 1 minute 57 seconds to complete this empty turnaround trek. My question is: Why don't they let people get on the train during this period? At least we would be moving. We have to stand there and wait for the empty train to leave the station and then return. It is only going into a dead-end tunnel. Why not let the people get on the train before it goes off into the tunnel?

The Queen's answer to anything that happens in Switzerland is simply, "The Swiss always have a logical reason. Always." She would rather not bother herself with these questions. I believed this for a long time, but the ninety-nine-step thing has forced me to re-think the Swiss. Maybe the whole system is falling apart. I want to know: What is this empty train thing all about?

I think the key to this dilemma is rooted in the Swiss culture, which, as I stated before, is based on being clean, exact, and on time. I can see no connection between the empty train situation and timeliness or exactness. However, sitting here in the plane, I think I have figured it out.

The key is cleanliness. I noticed that there is never a piece of paper, an empty bottle of pop, or any trash on these trains. I know they have a crew that cleans the trains every evening, but there should have been something left behind by the previous customers. The Swiss will tell you that they themselves do not litter, as they have too much pride. This train is in the airport, so many foreigners take it. They probably have left something behind.

I have pieced all this information together and solved the empty train puzzle. During the extra time that the train is in the tunnel, a SWAT cleaning team boards, cleans the train, and leaves. Any passengers would just slow them down, so passengers are not allowed to board the train.

My theory may have some holes in it, I admit, but I intend to do some fieldwork to prove it. I have devised a clever experiment. I will leave a piece of paper on a train, disembark, wait until it comes out of the tunnel, re-board, and see if my paper is still there. I will need to do this a few times to order to make a concrete deduction.

I think I will perform this experiment the next time I am in Zürich Airport. Oh, wait. On the next trip, in April, the Queen will be traveling with me. I dare not do it then, as she will start the obsessive-compulsive lecture again. Normally she doesn't mind these minor inconveniences, but since this will involve a few extra train trips and she will be jet-lagged, she could be a bit less understanding.

Maybe I'd better wait until I am traveling alone. Since I will need some extra time to perform the experiment, I may have to wait until next spring, when again I have that extra hour at the airport due to the time change.

Do you think I am spending too much time in Switzerland?

Sue the pasta!!

There is a very quaint little Italian restaurant in the Latin Quarter of Paris. It is a romantic place to dine. Susan and I found this gem one October when she accompanied me on a business trip to the City of Lights. The food was good, the prices reasonable, and, as an added benefit, the menu was in three languages.

It was a welcome break not to have to translate even the most basic foods. It is amazing how a simple thing like looking over the menu can become a chore if it is in a language you struggle with. This menu was in French, Italian, and English.

One dish was extremely rare. This is the only menu I have ever seen it on. Well, it may be very common in France and even Italy. We speak enough of these two languages to know that the both the Italian and French versions translated to "Pasta with avocados."

However, whoever did the English translation made a slight error. In French, as in many languages, there are words that are spelled the same but have different meanings. The French word *avocat* either means *avocado* or *advocate*. So in this little Italian restaurant in the Latin Quarter, within sight of Notre Dame, a pasta dish is listed on the menu in English as "Pasta with Lawyers." Somewhat romantic, isn't it?

4-26-06

My dad never flew in an airplane. He arrived in the Pacific to help his idol, MacArthur, retake the Philippines by way of a troop carrier ship.

He was a patient, quiet man who by the time I came along had only about 10 percent of the hearing he was born with. There was some dispute over how much of his hearing loss resulted from his war injuries and how much came from his profession, the printing of newspapers.

It was typical of my father that he never qualified for a military disability pension, because he never applied for one. In his view, he wasn't really disabled; others were worse off. Besides, it meant staying around to fill out paperwork. After all, in war, these things happen: People become deaf.

My father was not an opinionated man, but in his own way, he could make people around him understand when he did not approve of someone. A favorite expression in these cases was to refer to the person as a "happy little moron."

He was a man of faith and dedication, a lefthander who was forced to write righty when he was in grammar school. The youngest of six boys, he acquired the nickname "Slugger" by belting a home run that resulted in the loss of a baseball that one of his brothers had just bought. Playing with a new ball was a treat; losing it in the woods after the second pitch was unthinkable.

He hit that home run left-handed, by the way. In later years when my friends and I would play ball, we used his glove as second base. We had no left-handers among us: What else would we do with a lefty glove?

He never drove a car. In fact, in 1940 his cavalry unit was still riding horses. I have one of his horseshoes hanging on my basement wall to this day. When they mechanized his unit in 1941, he put in for a transfer, even though it meant he lost rank.

He did have a great sense of direction, so he was the constant navigator for my mother, the driver. This actually resulted in Mother never acquiring any sense of direction. After his death, she was often literally lost.

A printer by trade, the second brother to take up that profession, he was a graduate of the New York High School of Printing. I worked three summers as a printer's assistant with him in the *New York Post* composing room. I saw how others respected his ability. Both the High School of Printing and the methods that were used to produce newspapers in the '50s, '60s, and '70s are gone now—dinosaurs that succumbed to the digital age. He never got to see the new technology in action, but I am sure he would have disapproved. It meant less work for the union guys.

My father worshipped my mother. It was hard to tell where one's opinions ended and the other's began. They were in sync, mostly because my father was agreeable to my mother's wishes.

He was firm on many things: Always vote Democrat nationally and Republican in state elections. Never buy a non-union newspaper. Never cross a picket line. All baseball players born after about 1950 were minor league at best. He would have firm opinions about the legitimacy of Bobbie Bonds' assault on the Babe's record.

He smoked at one point, but he never drank, except for a beer on a hot day. He was born at home in 1919 and, with no religious reason to have it performed, he was not circumcised. I grew up knowing what an unsnipped man looked like.

My father never wrote in script. He only printed. I am not sure if this was a result of being switched in grade school from a left-hander to a right-hander. The only script I ever saw him use was his signature. I am similar; most of my letters are printed, with some script thrown in. Dad would consider this a penmanship sin. "Don't mix script and block letters, and don't mix upper- and lowercase letters." For some reason I once got into the habit of using one or two uppercase words within a lower case sentence. It was probably a method of rebellion on my part. When I do that now, I laugh, imagining what he would say.

I never realized until much later that he was never very happy living in his mother-in-law's house. He did all the maintenance and even paid the taxes, but it was not his house. As a child I just saw one big, happy family and didn't realize the quiet dynamics that were going on. My sisters, just that much older, understood more about this.

The early morning of October 21, 1944, dawned after my father had spent the night in a foxhole in the Philippines. He had waded ashore the previous day as part of the invasion force that started to retake the islands from the Japanese. In the distance, he could hear the naval battle between the Japanese and American fleets. If the American ships lost, he and his comrades knew that the Japanese ships would soon be off the beach shelling Allied positions. He must have thought that he might die that day. He didn't, but he did die of a heart attack thirty years later and was buried on October 21, 1974. Kind of ironic, I guess.

He never flew in an airplane, although he almost got to in 1944. A pilot acquaintance offered to take him up in 1943, but his unit was scrambled before that could happen.

Today, April 26, 2006, I am on a business class jet, with my Queen next to me. We just had a very nice steak and some wine. She chose the French, I took the South African: both reds, both very good, just what you would expect on an intercontinental business class flight. If Dad had gotten up in that plane in 1943, he would have had a totally different experience.

Why is today so special? As of today, I have been alive for 20,371 days: the exact number that my father lived. Tomorrow I outlive him. I estimate that as of today, I have spent well over a million miles in the air a result of working on one continent and living in another. My father never flew in an airplane.

Somehow I know I will never live what he lived. I am eternally grateful to that man who went about his daily routine in the silence of near-deafness—putting in his shift to get the news out to New York City, living in his mother-in-law's house—and who earned two Purple Hearts fighting for what he believed.

Firestarter meets Louis Vuitton

I have a cousin. Well, I have many cousins. I'm of Italian origin, you know. The one I am writing about here I'll call Cathy. I'll call her that mostly because that's her name. Wait a second; I have a number of cousins by that name. It doesn't help if I just focus on the first cousins; I think there are three or four with the name Cathy.

Maybe it's the Cathy who has a PhD from Princeton. No, wait— that's one of the other Cathys. Actually, she is a with-a-K Kathy. So that's not her. It could be the Cathy who is one of the twins. No, she's on the other side of the family. Maybe it's Cathy who lives outside of Boston and married Leonard. No, that's not the right one either.

Oh, yes, I remember: The Cathy I'm thinking about was raised by my mother after Cathy's mother got sick. I remember this young kid running around the house. That's her. Oh, yes. I also remember her burning down the same house. Well, not completely down, but it was one hell of a fire. Yup, that's the Cathy I am writing about.

When Cathy was not busy playing with matches, she was busy growing up to be the strong, independent woman who now has a loving husband and a daughter of her own. Her daughter's wedding is coming up next summer, so it's time for the generations to move forward.

Cathy herself would love to move forward, especially if *forward* means getting a Louis Vuitton bag. She always wanted one, and she told her husband Mark this very same thing.

The issue is that Cathy didn't *really* tell Mark what she *really* wanted, so how can you fault Mark? I don't mean to take the in-law side of the argument, but Mark is a man, so it seems, in this case, genitals are stronger than blood. Admittedly, I wasn't there for the discussion, but here is how it was told to me.

Cathy: "You know, I would like a Louis Vuitton bag."

Mark: "What's that?"

Cathy: "Those very distinctive and chic bags you see people have."

Mark: "Oh, the ones that they make knock-offs of?"

Cathy: "Yes, but I want a real one." (Points go to Cathy here for communicating right upfront that she isn't interested in a knock-off.)

Mark: "Okay, go buy one. If I get it for you it will be the wrong color or style, so you'd best get it yourself." (Great job on Mark's part. Not only does he ensure she will be satisfied, he takes himself out of the shopping trip.)

Cathy: "Well, I was thinking that it would best if I got one in Paris at the original store."

Mark: "Oh, yeah, that's a good idea. You know, your cousin Gerard is over there all the time, so send him a check and a description of what you want."

Now in his defense, Mark is not a traveler, so it would not be second nature for him to assume his wife was talking about a trip to Paris and not a bag. Of course, had she said she wanted to go to a *Star Wars* convention in Timbuktu, he would have booked the next plane. Mark is really into that stuff. One year's Christmas card pictured him and Cathy as Luke Skywalker and Princess Whomever. You can tell I am not a fan.

The conversation continued.

Cathy: "I was thinking that maybe we could go ourselves and get it together."

In fairness to Mark again, when presented with the request, "Let's go buy a purse together," most men realize that it is an invitation to say no so that the woman can have her peace and quiet while shopping.

This differs greatly from the request, "Let's go look at furniture together," which is a request to say yes and share the shopping experience. It all depends on what the item is. If it is personal girly stuff like stockings, underwear, or a purse, the right answer is "Go by yourself and enjoy." If it is a communal item where the wife is at least pretending to want the husband's input, like furniture, appliances, or paint colors, the right answer is, "I will gladly come." Mark thought it was the girly thing, so he said the following:

Mark: "Well, traveling alone could be an issue, so why not call Gerard and meet him in Paris the next time he goes?"

Cathy: "You imbecile. How unromantic can you get! I want to go to Paris with you. You're my husband. I don't want to go with a cousin. It could be a second honeymoon in the most romantic city in the world."

Mark, very sheepish now: "I thought we were talking about a pocketbook?"

This happened a while ago, so I'm sure Cathy has calmed down. Maybe, however, she's still mad? Knowing her history, if I were Mark, I'd go to bed with a fire extinguisher under my pillow.

8. Having a screw loose— maybe more than one

Odd habits,
OCD,
hypochondria,
and a unique way of looking at the world.

Loose Screws

The Queen was the first person who pointed out my slightly compulsive nature. I contend that she exaggerates this and that, in fact, she is the root cause of the minor amount of compulsions that I may have.

When we used to shop at the local video store, she would walk ahead of me and disturb the video boxes just enough that I had to stop and line them up again. She actually contends that this was done only to demonstrate that I have this problem and to assist me in overcoming it. I know that the reason she did it was to keep me busy rearranging the boxes, leaving her to make the choice of movie for the evening. No wonder we ended up with so many chick flicks.

Recently, under royal command, I painted the living room, dining room, and office. In one of my phone calls with a close friend, I told him about my paint job. He asked, "Did you line up the screws in the switch plates?" I have been doing my own renovations, large and small, for thirty-three years and never paid any attention to switch plate screws.

The screws that hold the switch plates and outlet covers are typically slot-headed screws. Some people, my friend informed me, make sure the slots are lined up in one direction after painting. Oh my God, I have been living in houses without lined-up plates my whole life.

After hanging up the phone, I went to the workshop to fetch a screwdriver and started correcting this terrible situation. First, I attended to the recently painted area. Then I started on the rest of the house. The Queen got a little annoyed when I moved the stove to adjust the outlet cover behind it. She really wasn't happy with my plan to move the fridge, and she made some type of obsessive-compulsive comment. So as not to prove her right, I decided not to do the fridge, but I made a mental note that when we sell the house I would make sure the fridge went along with the deal. I won't want the new owners to see we had misaligned screws.

I was about halfway through the realignment when it dawned on me: In which direction was I supposed to line up the screw slots: horizontally or vertically? I decided that all the screwhead slots in both switch plates and outlet covers should be horizontal.

It is a good thing that my sons-in-law were already in the family, for if they had been part of vertically aligned families, I would have had to have that old mixed-marriage conversation with the princesses. "You don't want to marry into a vertically aligned family, do you? How will you raise the kids?"

I am sure that my friend thought nothing of his comment. In fact, I am sure his switch plates are completely unaligned. Maybe he has screws on the same switch plate going at right angles to each other. He doesn't sweat the small stuff.

Now this whole sordid screw-alignment affair has brought out an interesting phenomenon. Switch plate screws don't stay aligned. I know that sounds strange. I even suspected that the Queen was running around the house misaligning my screws when I was out. Remember the video store?

I have come to accept that there must be a less diabolical explanation. Indeed, I have done tests and found that, if the screws are not tight enough, they can move slightly over time, causing misalignment. I mentioned this to the Queen one day, and she agreed, saying, "I think some of your screws are loose!"

Counting underwear

Between spring 2003, and fall 2007, I commuted from my home in Solon, Ohio, to Kemptthal, Switzerland, where my office and secretary were located. It was not as bad as you may think, since I always knew my schedule well in advance. I could plan the days I would be in Europe. Once I arrived in Switzerland, I usually stayed in the same hotel, my home away from home. I would remain set up in the hotel for one or two weeks at a time.

When you compare this to the travel schedule that many American executives have—numerous one-night trips or unannounced trips that always tend to conflict with family activities—mine was an easy travel life.

To facilitate this life style, I set up a complete duplicate wardrobe in Switzerland. I could travel back and forth with minimum luggage. My clothes were cleaned by the hotel and left in a cupboard in my office, ready for my return. Everything from socks to toiletries, shirts to ties, shoes to undershirts were left in Europe for my next trip.

The selection of clothes in Europe is not that good for someone my size, over 225 pounds. I buy most of my clothing in North America. I also had American preferences for items like toiletries and soap. I would not buy that much in Europe but instead bring over items as I needed them.

It was important to know exactly what I had there at any given time. Changes in season, formal dress requirements, and the fact that clothes wear out dictated that I know what I had in Europe.

I accomplished this with a simple Excel spreadsheet that listed all my belongings. It started out mostly as a clothes list, but in the end it was all-inclusive. Every personal item I had in Europe was listed, including a club-by-club list of golf clubs. I didn't want to be caught on a Swiss course without a three wood, did I?

I must say the list got a little out of hand near the end. It detailed almost everything about each item. For example, the quantity of dress shirts were identified as solid or stripe, plain or button-down, and of course by color. I had it down to a science, with a column that even alerted me to items I needed bring once the quantity went below a certain level.

The Queen was one of the few people who knew about my list, and she would shake her head when I brought it out while packing for a trip. She maintained that I was a little like the character Adrian Monk from the TV show. She even told a friend once, "Ask Gerard how many V-neck versus crew neck T-shirts he has in Switzerland."

I think it is rather normal for a person to have a spreadsheet detailing the status of his European underwear. Don't you?

My extra bone

I am a curler, not of hair, of which I have very little these days, but a curler on ice. I take part in that ancient sport invented by the Scots, where the goal is to slide a 42-pound piece of granite down the ice to a target 146 feet away. Curling has been an official Olympic sport since Nagano in 1998. The Queen and I learned it in Canada, where more than half of all the curlers in the world reside. I would rate my wife's abilities above mine in all areas but sweeping. My upper body strength gives me an edge there.

Most people think that the object is to throw the rock down the ice. That is not exactly the correct method. The proper form is to slide your body down the ice while holding the rock, then let the rock go at the proper point. You must push off with one foot while sliding on the other. The piece of wood or rubber that one pushes off from is called the *hack*. The push-off can range between a hard explosion and a gentle slide. It all depends on the ice conditions and the type of shot required.

I am very familiar with the ice and hacks in our club in a Cleveland suburb but rather unfamiliar with both at our sister club across town. The first time I was on their ice, I was the skip of our team, the quarterback. It was time for me to deliver my first stone, and I had to throw it hard. My goal was to knock out two of their rocks; the ice conditions called for a hard push-off.

The hack was slightly lower than I was used to. When I pushed off, my left foot slid down the ice the way it was supposed to, but my right foot flew out of the hack and straight up into the air. The effect was a 180-degree split.

Splits may seem very graceful when gymnasts or ice dancers do them, but for a fifty-plus-year-old man, splits are not recommended. I felt and heard my tendon pop. Here is a great rule of thumb I learned that day: Whenever you hear a loud pop coming from your groin, it is not good.

They carried me off the rink, and I iced the area where my right leg meets my body. It was painful, but the ice helped keep the swelling down, and with a few Advil, the injury seemed healed enough that I could walk by the next day. So I took my flight to Dallas for a business meeting there.

All went well until I took my pants off that evening in the Dallas hotel. I noticed that my right thigh was purple and then, to my horror, that the purple color went as far as my family jewels. To be more specific, only half of the jewels had changed color, the right half. One was now a ruby, while the other was still a pearl. Not in size, mind you, but in color. After a few weeks the color faded, and my physician informed me that I had a partially ripped the tendon in my groin.

Fast-forward about five months. I was in the shower when I noticed that the right side of my groin felt different from the left. I wondered if this had always been the case. It felt like my pelvic bone was larger on the right side. Since my annual physical was coming up, I put this on the list to discuss with my doctor. It actually felt like an extra bone had grown in my groin.

I didn't have much concern about the effect on my body. After all, I was playing golf, power walking, doing all the things I normally do, with no ill effect. My biggest concern was a copyright issue. Indeed, if this were an extra bone, would it be named after me? I could see it now in the medical journals: "A very small number of people have the right-side-pelvic-anterior bone, often called the Tortorelli bone." I would get into the medical journals. It might even make getting my book published a lot easier. The title I had picked was *Loose Screws*, but I could be convinced to call it *The Tortorelli Bone* if it made the publishers take notice.

So at my physical, I asked my doctor if I did have an extra bone and he discovered it, would it be named after him or me? My doc knows me well and knows that I am a part-time hypochondriac who thinks every ailment I have is an undiscovered disease. He was almost ready for the question. He assured me that if this were a new bone, he would not contest it being named the Tortorelli Bone.

With that assurance in hand, I let him feel my crotch. (I ask the reader not to quote the last sentence out of context.) At first, he couldn't feel it at all. Then, after I insisted, he acknowledged that he felt it, but it was slight and "probably nothing" and "had always been there." He mentioned that we are not made symmetrically. When I reminded him about the injury, he did admit it could be a calcification at the injured spot. I thought he was just humoring me.

A few months later, I had a CAT scan because of an unrelated abdominal problem. The abdominal issue turned out to be nothing, but my doc called anyway to tell me that indeed I had a calcification at the site of the tendon rip. He wouldn't call it an extra bone, but what else would a bunch of calcium in your body be? I think he was probably annoyed that he had given up the naming rights to this new bone. In any event, it was now documented.

Eight years later, the extra bone is still there. No one from any of the medical book publishing houses has called. I guess I will not get into the medical books after all. However, my extra bone may help if my body ever has to be identified after some horrific accident. I can see the headlines now: "Dental records not available, body identified by abnormalities of the groin."

Medical school

You may wonder whether this piece has something to do with my daughter's time at medical school. It doesn't. The way I figure it, she can write her own book. I want to tell you about my medical school experience. I never actually went to medical school—at least not the kind where you go to classes and study.

I claim to have learned a lot just by going to my doctor and asking questions. In fact, if it were possible to glean your way to a medical degree, I'd have one now. My doctor knows I am a part-time hypochondriac, so he spends a good deal of time explaining what is going on in my body, to help prevent me from coming up with my own scenarios. We have a good relationship that way.

It all started when I first moved down to Ohio from Canada. I went to him, as a friend had recommended him. My first visit was quite successful. We established a good rapport, although he was a bit confused by the cholesterol data I had brought down from my Canadian doctor. In Canada, cholesterol is measured in mille moles, where in the United States milligrams are used. My Canadian data showed my cholesterol at 6.5, which I calculated to be slightly over 1,000 in U.S. terms. This meant either I could be used as a national oil reserve or I did the calculation wrong. In any event, we thought it better to retake the tests rather than rely on my data conversion skills.

Soon after my second appointment with the doctor, I went on a tour of the local gym. Low and behold, he was there taking a shower. I guess I should have been ready for the odd looks when I said, "Hi, doc, I finally get to see *you* naked."

My real training as a GP came during my annual physicals. I always have mine during December. I have the time then, and it gets me in a good mindset for the upcoming year. About eight years ago, while the nurse was taking my vitals, she asked if I would mind if a med student took part in the physical. I said I didn't mind. The nurse then said, "Okay, she will be with you soon." No big deal, I have had woman docs before, and, after all, my daughter was a med student, so in a way I was showing solidarity.

The beauty of having a med student take part is that the doctor explains everything to her or him, and you get a free education. The bad part is that all the procedures have to be done twice.

That first year I learned two important things. The first was during the prostate exam. For those of you who don't know, this is done by feeling the prostate through the rectum. This was one of those doing-it-twice parts that was not all that great. It turned out that this was this student's first prostate exam, so she probably had no idea if things were okay or not. The doctor explained that "in his day," they told med students that if the prostate felt like an ear lobe it was fine. If it felt like the tip of your nose, it was bad. I must have had an "ear lobe" prostate, because I was given a clean bill of health.

The second thing I learned was the turn your head and cough thing. You see, the med student said, "Turn your head and cough." She then did her thing with one of the family jewels. Then she said, "Turn your head the other way and cough." and proceeded to do her thing with the other. My doctor stopped her and asked, "Why do we ask patients to turn their head?" She started to try to answer and then decided she should admit, "I don't know." Well, it turns out that this is done so patients don't cough on the doctor. So asking me to turn the other way had no significance. I was learning quickly, without paying a cent in med school tuition.

Fast forward to the next year's exam: another med student, this time a male. Again double tests were performed. Now, however, I was armed with knowledge. While the med student was preparing for the prostate exam, I asked him if he knew about the ear lobe versus nose tip analogy. Then I explained what I had learned the previous year. He looked at me disbelievingly, but my doc told him I was right. Some nerve this guy had! I'm trying to teach him, even letting him poke his fingers into private places, and he questions my advice! I should have charged him a consultation fee.

I have a good friend who is an ENT surgeon. The *E* and *N* stand for "ear" and "nose" respectively, so I figured he'd be an expert in this ear lobe versus nose tip analogy. Funny, he didn't know anything about it. You would think he would. Maybe my doc made the whole thing up. I'd better check his diploma next visit.

The dating game at 35,000 feet

Sometimes I write my stories in Switzerland, sometimes in the United States. This little observation is being written somewhere southwest of Iceland at 35,000 feet above the Atlantic. I figure I am not too far away from the resting place of the Titanic. I came to the realization that I am about as far above the ocean surface as the famed wreck is below.

This started me thinking about the last days on board the unsinkable ship. You can't help but think of the movie and the found and then lost love that was the main plot. How many real characters met someone for the first time on board? Did they fall in love? Were they rescued, to live happily ever after?

By comparison, my eight-hour journey across the Atlantic is quite boring, one of about thirty transatlantic flights I'll take this year, because I live in Solon, Ohio, and my office is outside of Zürich.

To help pass the time, I decide to play a mental game of matchmaker. Suppose one of the women on this flight is looking to meet someone. How would I stack up against my competition? I have it on good authority from a guy who spent two years in the seminary that this type of daydreaming does not constitute any form of infidelity. After all, it is just fantasy.

How many women on this plane would even be interested in me? I happen to be sitting in business class, which is full, while the back of the plane is empty. They have more room in coach for a quarter of the price.

Of the thirty business class seats, twenty-seven are filled with men and three with women. That's a nine-to-one ratio. This is an unusually high men-to-women ratio, so my competition is tough. The ratio probably says something about executives and the glass ceiling, but I'll leave that for another story.

The three women in business class are mixed in both age and status. There is a thirty-something business women, dressed for travel in jeans, pullover, and comfy shoes. There is a slightly older, more dignified-looking woman with just the right amount of makeup and some type of designer outfit. Lastly is a middle-aged, wrinkled-from-years-of-smoking type who is traveling with her husband. He is quite old.

I looked around at my competition, the other twenty-six men, and eliminated the guy traveling with his wife for obvious reasons. Of course, I had to eliminate his wife for the same reasons. Now this brings the ratio to twenty-six to two. It's getting worse.

It seems that most of the business class seats are filled with old men. The guy next to me is in his thirties, but the rest appear to be my father's age. With further examination, I observe that two or three men are better looking than me. Now we're talking. There're only four of us still in the running, vying for two women. One looks like he has a bad personality, so I know I can beat him. Hey, even I will resort to personality if I can get an edge.

Now it's down to three to two. I think I can take the guy in the corduroy, based just on fashion. And now we are at parity. Judging my lone remaining competitor, I give him a seven and me a nine (I am morally against giving myself a ten). Therefore, in my mind, I am the best catch in the business class section of this 767, giving me my choice of women. That brings up another problem. How do I choose between the two women? I wonder if they would mind me holding a swimsuit competition.

After all this mental exercise, I have to go to the washroom. I am not sure whether the thinking made me have to go or if it was the Diet Coke. Airplane washrooms are quite small. You really get close and personal with your mirror image. Then I see this old guy, about my father's age, staring back at me from the other side of the mirror. I assume he's one of the old geezers from business class who is lost somewhere inside the wall of the washroom. Then I realize: He is me!

Come to think of it, in two months I will be the age my father was when he died. That's the oldest I remember him. All of a sudden, I wasn't so sure how I would fare versus the competition. Maybe even the corduroy guy might beat me. How did this happen? Look, if the twenty-six others in business class want to get old, that's their lives. This is mine.

Maybe the smoker lady would like to share a cigarette later. I don't smoke, but if it makes me look cool at this age, I can always start. I would have to figure out what to do with her old husband. You know, I think he actually looks younger than I do.

What's in a name, anyway

I have learned that a name is the most valued possession that anyone has. It is who you are to the world. It is something that says *you*. That is why it is such a social sin when we call someone by the wrong name.

I feel comfortable with certain people having certain names. I have a friend named Gary. He is a Gary, and in my mind, he looks like a Gary should look like. If I meet another Gary who deviates a lot from him, I may comment to the Queen, "He doesn't look like a Gary."

Then there are the people who have two names in common use. I fall into this category, as my family all call me by my legal American name, Gerard. The rest of the world calls me Gerry. The Gerry name developed in high school and even that evolved: first it was spelled Jerry. I changed the *J* to *G* because the *G* gave me the same initials as my real name. Besides *J* is just not me—not round enough.

On my Canadian passport, my name is spelled Gerrard, while my American legal name is Gerard. The Canadian moniker is a result of a misspelling at the time we immigrated to Canada in 1985.

Some people have an official nickname that changes with time. My cousin Victor is a case in point. The nickname given to him by his brother many years ago is Fuzzy. I think there is a rule that you can't call a guy Fuzzy if he has a PhD from Princeton, so he became just Fuzz, although it does, I think, say Victor on his diploma.

Victor is actually a good example of another situation: a nickname that is used only by a small group of people. My princesses first met Victor when they were five and three years old during a Christmas trip back to the states. Since they had never heard of such a name and since we had been reading the "Night before Christmas" poem, they decided his name must be Vixen. When I would mention Victor, they would say, "Oh, you mean Vixen." I guess there is no rule at Princeton about reindeer names.

How important is a name? Would your life be different if you had been given another name? Up until a few months before I was born, my mother intended for me to be named Mark Damian. This name is kind of exotic and sexy at the same time. Although the Damian part reminds me of the leper priest in Molokai, it has impact because of the combination with Mark—a little like Mark Anthony. Could you imagine Elizabeth Taylor calling Richard Burton just plain Mark? I would insist on always having them together: Mark Damian. I wonder what my life would have been like had that actually been my name.

The Mark Damian moniker was changed in honor of my grandfather, who had died just months before I was born. I am told this was my father's wish. This was impressive, because it was my mother's father who died, not my father's.

So there I was, Gerard Francis, a.k.a. Jerry, then a.k.a. Gerry, destined to have a less sexy name, but I chalk that sacrifice up to family harmony. Everyone has to do his part.

I never met a Mark Damian, but if I ever do, I bet he'll look a lot like Richard Burton.

9. Oh, the holidays

In the Bronx, there used to be an elevated subway train[9] (what New Yorkers call the "el") running above Gun Hill Road between White Plains Avenue and Webster Avenue. They tore it down sometime in the '80s. Now, whenever I see that area, I think of Christmas, because there is no el.

---

9   Only a New Yorker would understand the paradoxical term "elevated subway."

Halloween: The mother
and child reunion

Halloween has come a long way. It was always a holiday we enjoyed, but now it's big business. It has even made its way to Europe, where at least the Swiss and Italians are starting to have some good old American fun on the last day of October.

As a kid we had a good time. I don't remember having to check our candy as rigorously for tampering as today's parents must, but the 1950s were a simpler and safer time.

With the costume party, what they call a "fancy dress party" in the UK, our teenage years took on a new Halloween interest. Having three friends with October birthdays, it seemed that this was a good month—and excuse—for a party. And I can recall a number of costume parties even after we were married. These were memorable for the costumes themselves, not the parties. In the late 1970s, the Cone Heads costume was a success, while a guy as a nun was always good too. The first year I worked for a candy bar company, Sue and I went as Crunch bars.

As kids came along, we experienced Halloween through our children, making costumes out of whatever was around and whatever was in vogue. I was in charge of taking them out on Halloween night. Since we lived in Canada during their trick or treating days, it was usually a rather cold experience.

Fast forward to today, October 13, 2006, a Friday—the 13th, by the way. I know it is a long way from Halloween still, but for some reason I decided that today would be a great day to carve a pumpkin. Oh, I must add that I am visiting my mother in a suburb of New York. She is on hospice care in her home. She needs oxygen full-time and takes a shot of morphine four or five times a day, but her spirits are good.

I decided that we should carve a pumpkin. The live-in hospice worker is from Ghana, so she was a little confused by what we were doing. After a while, she went to her room.

My mother never took a large part in holiday customs when we were kids. That was my father's domain. He had his own systems, whether decorating the Christmas tree, coloring Easter eggs, or carving a pumpkin. My dad knew the way to do it—his way. My mother let him because he enjoyed it so much. So to say this was the first time I carved a pumpkin with my mom, me in my fifty-seventh year and her in her ninetieth, was not an exaggeration.

I wasn't sure how she would take it. At first she gave me an "Are you crazy? What do we need a pumpkin for?" look. Then she instructed me on which knife to use. "Get the sharp one. No, not that one; the one with the black handle."

I asked her to draw what she wanted to carve on a piece of paper and while she complained, she made a reasonable likeness of what I will call the traditional triangular eyes, nose, and serrated mouth Jack-o-lantern design. That's what I set out to do. After copying her design on to the pumpkin, I was ready to cut. But wait—Mom informed me that the nose was too small, the mouth was too large, the eyes were too far apart. Hey, was this the spirit of my father living in my mom's body.

We both felt accomplished that evening, almost nostalgic. As I looked back through the dark on the way to my car, I could see our creation, lit by three candles, smiling at me.

Two days later I called her from back in Ohio. She surprised me with a new remark. "Were you trying to kill us with that pumpkin?"

I could tell she was relishing what she was about to say. She continued, "I am on oxygen. The candles could have started an explosion."

We hadn't thought of that at the time. She laughed. I laughed. And somewhere, my father was shaking his head.

Some gloves, a bowling ball, and ironed shirts

Remember when your kids made something in craft class at school as a present for you at Christmas? Sadly, these are treasures that we often discard as time goes by. I bet if you had saved some of these items and presented them back to the now grown-up gift-givers, they would enjoy them more than most other presents. It would be a reminder of their youth.

I remember one item from my grammar school days that I had made for my mother. Since no one was a smoker in my family, an ashtray, which was the standard fare in the '50s, was not something that I made. The memorable item was, in fact, a jewelry box. The ingredients were a cigar box, some satin-type material, some cotton balls, glue, some paint, and an assortment of pasta. In my opinion, the result was exquisite enough to house the crown jewels of England.

The inside was padded. The cotton balls covered with the satin material would protect my mom's precious stones. Green paint covered the outside. A few coats were needed, as I remember, to cover the White Owl logo. The top was the thing that gave it life. I chose pasta shells, the small ones, to glue on top of the green cigar box. There was a border around the perimeter of shells glued end to end. In the middle of the cover, I chose to use shells again to spell MOM. I remember that she thought that was the greatest gift she had ever received when I gave it to her.

A few months later, I remember noticing that one or two of the shells had fallen off and were nowhere to be found. About two years later I noticed the box itself was gone. Enough time had elapsed that I understood that this was how life worked. Things once treasured get discarded.

This recently got me thinking about the presents that my kids have made for us. The Queen and I are hoarders, so we still have many of them. They are buried somewhere in the basement next to a cheese grater and a three-foot high statue of a man picking his nose, which are subjects for their own stories.

It also got me to thinking about the presents I have given Susan during our life together. Some were memorable, some not so. Some were expensive, some as cheap as dirt. The cost was never a function of the amount of love we shared but of the amount of money we had at the time.

It all started with the pair of leather gloves she gave me one Christmas in high school when we went to see the Fred McMurray movie *Follow Me, Boys* at Radio City Music Hall. We exchanged presents while standing in line for the show. Standing in line at Radio City was a New York tradition. I had gotten her a bottle of some type of smelly stuff based on what her friend told me she liked.

I remember two major things about this first present exchange. I was sure she spent a lot more on me than I did on her, and the gloves were too big. I had to keep both of these conclusions to myself, especially the size of the gloves. I understood at the time that the size of a man's hands was an indication of the size of something else. No need for her to suspect anything she didn't need to know. This was only high school, after all.

I remember nothing more about Christmas presents until our engagement. We exchanged rings at Christmas in 1970. She gave me my class ring, and I gave her the engagement ring. This was done in the bar of the Plaza Hotel in New York. When they closed the Plaza a few years ago, I felt old.

For our first married Christmas, I surprised her with one of the most memorable gifts. We didn't have much money to spend, nor did we need much, having just gotten married five months earlier. Between the wedding showers and engagement parties, what else could we need?

I was intent on finding a gift that would be the basis of an activity that we could do together. This was going to be the beginning of a life pursuit where we could be together and enjoy each other's company. When the friend I was shopping with and I met up in front of the checkout, I proudly showed him what I had chosen. His reaction was, "I didn't know Susan was a bowler?" My response: "She isn't, but we can start in our married life." I can still see the look on his face.

The bowling ball and bag lasted in the family from 1972 until 1997, when we moved from Toronto to Cleveland. Sue held a garage sale and, alas, the bowling ball and bag was priced at five Canadian dollars. A friend of ours who was helping with the sale demanded the asking price because of sentimental value. When the guy offered $2.50, she said she would take it but only if he listened to the "first Christmas present" story. She then regaled him with my tale. I can just imagine this fellow telling his friends over a cold Labatt's: "You can't believe what this guy gave his wife for their first Christmas, eh?"

I still maintain this was the greatest present ever. Not because we took up bowling with Susan's new ball, bag, and shoes. We only stayed in the league a few weeks. It was because Susan will always remember what I gave her our first Christmas together. When asked, most married couples do not remember their first Christmas presents.

I can't remember most of the other Christmas presents that I gave my wife in the thirty-seven years we have been married. But one other stands out. During Christmas in 1983, we were living in the French-speaking part of Switzerland. For the first time in my career, I had a job that required me to wear a jacket and tie every day. We could not afford to send shirts out to be done. My gift was that I would do the ironing of my shirts for the entire year.

That accomplished a few things. I got to walk a mile in Sue's shoes. She had more time to spend with the princesses. And I got to learn how to iron a shirt. Three benefits in one gift. I don't know where you can get such value, except in a bowling ball, bag, and shoes.

How can I outdo this present for future Christmases? Next year I'm thinking about a painted cigar box with pasta glued to the top.

Christmas traditions

Pieces of Dead Animals

My father was a quiet man who was firm in his traditions. I don't know where this particular tradition came from, but he followed it religiously. He always made a point to keep the wishbone from the Thanksgiving Day turkey and hang it on the Christmas tree. Ideally, it was the first ornament hung on the tree.

The year that Mom decided not to have turkey for Thanksgiving, my dad really showed his stuff. Because we were having turkey for Christmas, two turkeys within five weeks of each other was deemed excessively fowl. We had a canned ham for Thanksgiving. Not to be deterred, Dad saved the key that opened the can, complete with the metal strip now wrapped around it, and hung that on the tree. Actually, it was quite pretty and almost fit in with the other ornaments.

Over the years, the wishbone on the tree tradition has met with different responses. The Queen's reaction on our first Christmas was, "Now tell me this again. You want to hang a piece of a dead animal on my Christmas tree?" She knows how to cut to the chase.

Friends in Canada actually gave me a Christmas tie with four wishbones glued to it. I never wore it. I still have it, though. This same couple, being concerned that our tree display a balanced diet, also gave us an ornament made from real Brussels sprouts. That I don't have any longer.

Painted Wood

That first Christmas, Sue found a paint-your-own balsa wood set of ornaments in a magazine and sent away for it. These were very simple pre-cut ornaments, about fifty in the set. All were different pre-drawn designs, like a coloring book, so all we had to do was paint between the lines. I took this up as a project, and by Christmas, we had some of our own ornaments. Since they are indestructible and travel well, we have almost all of the originals to this day. We have used them on every tree in all parts of the world. Some even have chew marks from our first puppy, Pepper, which make them even more special.

In 1972, we were asked to be godparents for our neighbor's first child, Melinda. One of the ornaments I colored, the one of a rocking horse, has "Melinda 1972" painted along the rocker. Twenty-two years later, I sent it to her. I don't know if she kept it, but I hope she did.

Sometimes Having a Choice Is Overrated

The first Christmas that we were in Europe, we had assumed we would be getting a Christmas tree and were told that the "fire brigade" would be selling them as a fundraiser. We expected to go to the firehouse one day, where we would find a multitude of trees, and we would browse for between fifteen minutes to half an hour, depending on how cold it was, and pick out a tree. That would be taking an American attitude to a Swiss situation.

The way it worked was a bit simpler. One night the wife of the captain of the fire brigade came to our door and asked in German, "Do you want a Christmas tree?" We said yes and she disappeared, only to return in three minutes with a "Tannenbaum." She handed it to us without much fanfare and said, "Thirty francs." Ah, the Swiss— simplicity at its best.

"Edward Scissor Hands" to "Laura, Butter Knife Hands"

As long as I can remember, my sister Laura, the one who doesn't clean, had wrapped the Christmas presents. She is an expert. She has never used scissors—never. She always uses a plain butter knife. She would fold the paper and zap, the butter knife would slide through it like, well, a knife through butter, every cut straight as an arrow. I always linked this to my dad, who was a printer and knew his way around paper.

This year I tried this same procedure. Thank God, most of the people who get to enjoy our presents are the "rip them open and don't save the paper" variety. It would be embarrassing for them to see how badly the paper was cut.

Little Christmas and Three Kings Cake

January 6 is the traditional day to celebrate the Epiphany, the visit of the Magi to the newborn Christ child. When I was growing up, this was called "little Christmas." We always received a present that was "brought by the Magi." No gold, frankincense, or myrrh, but some small, unwrapped present was placed on the kitchen table. This tradition did not survive adulthood, and as far as I can remember, I got my last Magi gift at about twelve years old.

A new tradition took its place in Switzerland, however: the Three Kings cake. We would bake a coin into a cake. Usually it would be a ten rappen coin, about the size of a dime and equivalent to eight U.S. cents. Whoever got the piece with the ten rappen coin was "King for the day" and did not have to do any chores. We followed this custom with the same coin for six years, even after we returned to North America. We still have it among the Christmas decorations, with a note attached listing who won it each year. In Switzerland, you can buy cakes with a toy baked into them, but we did our own.

When Is Christmas Not a Holiday?

Enter the Swiss. When the Swiss are not shooting apples off their sons' heads, they are busy calculating how to minimize holiday time for employees. Please understand that even new employees in Switzerland get four weeks of vacation, so no one is starved for time off. However, for those of us who consider Christmas sacred and time off at Christmas sacrosanct, the Swiss are nothing short of heretics.

The Swiss agree that you should get Christmas and the day after off. On the surface, that's not a bad policy. If Christmas falls on a Monday, both Monday and Tuesday are free from the confines of work. You will *not* work on Christmas or the day after Christmas! They are rigid about that—so rigid that when Christmas is a Saturday, as it was in 2004, you will not work on Christmas or the day after. Therefore, if you were a worker in Switzerland in 2004, you got the 25th and the 26th off. Don't blame the company if it happened to be a Saturday and Sunday that year. You were expected at work on Friday and Monday. Today, some twenty-five years after I first moved to Switzerland, many companies gave a half day off on the 24th.

There is good with the bad. In Switzerland, the Christ child comes on Christmas Day, not Santa Claus. Santa (in Swiss German he is called Sami Klaus) comes on December 6, St Nicholas Day. He brings the kids nuts, tangerines, and some candy. The Christ child brings presents. So maybe they don't have it so mixed up after all.

The eight weeks of Advent

I know what you must be thinking, but no, I did not fail Catholic studies when I was in grade school. In fact, I received an award for having the highest marks in "religion class," as we called it then. I do know that there are four weeks in Advent, the preparatory time before Christmas.

Even if I didn't know that from my school days, it would be hard not to glean it from all the Advent wreaths that one sees in Europe, not just in churches but in hotel lobbies, businesses, stores, and in many other public areas. Not that the Europeans are that religious: These wreaths are just a cultural thing. The Europeans use four candles of the same color, while the Catholic Church uses a pink candle for the third Sunday of Advent. All the others are purple or dark red. I used to know the liturgical reason for that, but I have forgotten. I hope they don't ask for my religion award back!

I am very aware that there are four weeks in Advent. My sister needs a refresher, however. It is January 19, 2006, and I am visiting in her home—a home that still has its Christmas tree up. This is not through error or because of lack of time to take it down. It is by design. My sister's birthday is January 16, and as a child she insisted that we keep the decorations up until that time. She has continued this tradition to this very day. She is the Energizer Bunny of the Christmas season: It just keeps on going and going.

My sister was quite a stickler for facts when she was younger. I remember her insisting that the three wise men and their camel herder should not be in the manger until January 6, the Epiphany. Once she put them on the other side of the room and moved them closer to the crib each day. During the time when their sojourn found them in the middle of the living room, the camel was knocked over and chipped. Hey, maybe she knew back then that Mom would give the set to me so she did this to ruin one of the pieces. Who knows, but I think of my sister whenever I see the camel. (That didn't come out right.)

As a couple, we gravitate toward the "early to decorate: early to undecorate" mantra. We usually decorate on Thanksgiving weekend. We don't put up the tree, which comes much later. You see, we still get a live tree. Well, I guess it is dead by the time we get it home, but it was live at one point. Our tradition is to keep the decorations until January 6, the Epiphany. We don't move the camel across the room. He's suffered enough.

We decorate the rest of the house early and the tree later. Decorating takes up a full day and a half before the tree goes up. We have Christmas plates and glasses that replace the regular ones, numerous wall decorations, wreaths for all the doors, table runners, place mats, and five nativity sets acquired over the years. You get the picture. All of this requires that the non-Christmas items that reside with us for the other eleven months of the year be packed away. It's a long but very enjoyable process.

My assistant in Switzerland heard me talk about the amount we decorated and was interested in how it looked. Last year I took photos of the house inside and out. She was impressed with the extent of the decorations.

She caught her breath, however, when she saw the candles I have in the front eight windows of the house. She started to laugh and called in a colleague, who was shocked when he heard it was my house in the picture. In Switzerland, where brothels are legal, a red candle in the window means that the woman in that room is "not busy" at the moment. I knew this as a fable, but it actually still exists. This year I put orange lights in the window; they look more like flames anyway. Oh, and I took them down right after Christmas.

Postscript: It is March 31, 2007: the day before Palm Sunday, eight days before Easter. I am sitting in my sister's house at the dining room table, looking at the manger set that is still in its place of honor on the mantel. She informed me that she was starting a new tradition—keeping the manger set up until Easter: the baby Jesus, the shepherds, the wise men, and even the camel.

I know what I am about to write sounds sacrilegious, but I suggested that at that rate, all she need do for Good Friday is take the baby Jesus out of the crib and nail him up on the wall. I think she said a prayer for my soul after that comment.

The Browns and the van Pelts

At the same time that we moved to Ohio, we became empty nesters. Although the kids come to visit at the holidays, they have lives in other places and can only stay a short while. Christmas is a time when the house should be filled with your family, especially children.

To help fill in this void during the holidays, we have invited four children to visit us every year since we arrived in Ohio. They come to our home during the Christmas season and bring cheer and good will to our guests and us. We know they have parents, but they don't come along. Every year it is the same four children, the two van Pelt kids and the two Brown kids. It wouldn't be an Ohio Christmas for us without them.

Even my neighbors get excited when they see them arrive. The first year they came, a neighbor I hardly knew stopped by just to see them and chat for a while. He had a smile on his face the entire time.

We have had our share of mishaps when they are here. One year the younger van Pelt fell, severely injuring his neck. After some therapy, he was right as rain by the time we saw him the following Christmas. Another time we thought we had lost his sister in a snowstorm, but a neighbor's kid found her under the fir tree in the front yard.

For some reason the two Brown kids haven't gotten into that many predicaments over the years. They do bring their pet, however, and for some Christmas seasons, their pet has brought a friend, kind of a pet of a pet. Their dog doesn't cause any problems. Just the contrary; he doesn't have much ambition. Not the run and fetch type at all. He'd rather relax all day.

To be honest, they spend a lot of time with us. It's usually not just an afternoon visit. This year, for instance, they were with us from right after Thanksgiving through New Year. The neighbors have come to know them and would miss them if they were to skip a year. Occasionally one of the neighbors actually sees them during the summertime. If that happens, I downplay the fact that they are in my home all year.

You see, it is usually Thanksgiving weekend when I take the homemade four-foot-high wood figures of Lucy and Linus van Pelt and Sally and Charlie Brown out of the garage and erect them on the lawn. Their dog is always lying on top of his doghouse, and his friend Woodstock, who was lost for a few years, is now back. Some people like cashews, others walnuts, but to me it wouldn't be a Tortorelli Christmas without some *Peanuts*.

Epilogue

Never-ending stories

Well, we have almost come to the end of this book odyssey. I honestly had to force myself to stop. There are so many stories to tell that I could go on for a few hundred more pages. I can't explain why I chose the stories that I did. Others might be funnier or carry more of a life lesson.

I do know that I left out some anecdotes because they were too embarrassing, like the time I lost my oldest in a department store when she was fifteen months old. Others I left out because they are too frightening to recall, like the time we lost our youngest in Venice when she was three. Don't worry, we got them back, both times. It was poetic justice that we lost both. Neither can claim, "You like her better. You didn't lose her."

I have a short list of the ones I want to publish next. I will try to make it a very eclectic book made up of a number of genres. Here is a sampling of what I mean.

- A business book, detailing a get-rich scheme for importing real Swiss Alps into the United States
- A how-to book, regaling the reader with how to have six orgasms in a cave (contains no sex)
- A true crime book, including the tale of smuggling Cuban cigars into the United States
- A cook book, with the famous stuffed lentils recipe, a Tortorelli delicacy
- And a book on collecting cutlery, Swiss-style, telling the Saga of the Vevey Spoon.

With the presence of our granddaughter Katelyn and the impeding birth of our grandson, Zorba, I will have a new source of anecdotes to draw from. Zorba is not his real name. Since his father is Greek, the Queen thought it a good name to use for him in his yet-to-be-born state.

Yes, I may have to write another book. Whether I do or not, I have already learned one thing that will stick with me forever. Life is always an adventure, and if you look at it the right way, it is an adventure worth retelling.

So I guess all I have left to do is sign off. I bet I can even make that a story.

The sign-off line...

It is a traumatic experience when your kids leave home, even under good circumstances. It was no exception when our younger princess spent the second half of grade eleven in France. We were living in Canada at the time. A few months later, the older princess went away to college. She was only three hours away, but she was still away. Let's face it: When they go away to college, it is often forever.

That was 1996, and we were just becoming Internet literate. We would be able to communicate via e-mail. Even at that time, one could feel that this new medium was a bit impersonal. What was needed was a heartfelt constant that could be used every time. It was then that I decided to have a sign-off line for my kids' e-mails.

It's been over thirteen years since I started this custom. I have used it for both daughters, whether they were at school in Ontario, Indiana, or France. It is used today when I send an e-mail to their homes or to their work addresses. I end my e-mail messages to them in the same manner. I must admit this is a private thing. I use it only when the e-mail is to them. If an e-mail goes to multiple recipients, I do not sign off this way. I consider it a show of respect that I include my two sons-in-law in this custom.

I don't think they ever realized how much thought went into developing this e-mail good-bye. The idea partly grew from what my mother used to say whenever we left the house. She would say, "Be careful." I came to realize that my mother was always afraid of life in some way. She thought of what could go wrong. A car could hit you. You could be mugged. You could fall down while carrying the proverbial stick and poke your eye out. Her way of dealing with this was to say, "Be careful." In the days before Internet, when we all lived in the same house, this was my mother's sign-off line.

I am my mother's child, and I worry about my kids—maybe in a more modern way, with less of the fearful worry but as much concern. I didn't want my sign-off line to sound like I didn't trust them or for it to show any fear. I did want it to relay that I wished all the best for them and that they were in my thoughts.

Since I started sending my daughters e-mails more than thirteen years ago, I have ended each e-mail with these simple words, which were the original working title for this book. I changed the title, but I think it is a good way to end the book in any case. All I have to do is change my name from *Dad* to *Gerry* …

Stay well, love always,

Gerry

LaVergne, TN USA
25 October 2009
161898LV00004B/1/P

9 781440 170690